FAITH, HOPE AND CHARITY

FAITH, HOPE AND CHARITY
The Defence of Malta

Kenneth Poolman

A Goodall paperback
from
Crécy Publishing Limited

First published in the UK in 1954 by William Kimber & Co Ltd
Republished in 2004 by Cerberus Publishing Limited
This edition first published in 2009 by Crécy Publishing Limited

ISBN 9 780907 579632

Printed and bound in Malta by Progress Press

A Goodall paperback

published by

Crécy Publishing Limited
1a Ringway Trading Estate, Shadowmoss Road, Manchester M22 5LH
www.crecy.co.uk

Contents

Acknowledgments

I wish to thank all the members of the Royal Air Force and Royal Navy, past and present, who have given so much of their time and interest towards the preparation of this book, particularly Wing Commander George Burges, Wing Commander John Waters, Wing Commander Peter Hartley, Wing Commander G. A. V. Collins and Wing Commander F. H. Dimmer.

All these officers played distinguished parts in the events described in the following pages, and without their kind help the telling of the story would have been impossible.

I also wish to thank Mr D. Hornsey at the Air Ministry and Mr Reg Holmes of the Department of Naval Information for their very great help in the gathering of material for the book.

Kenneth Poolman

CHAPTER ONE

The Pattern

'*Mi son sbrigato della savorra,*' said the pilot. The intercom answered him, thin and angry.

'*Hai lanciato sul mare, scemo.*'

'*Lo so, lo so.*'

Effi Ciantar, announcer for the Rediffusion Company, was listening in over the ultra short-wave.

'I've dropped my bombs.'

'They went in the sea.'

'I know, I know.'

Ciantar listened hard and smiled grimly to himself as the distorted chatter went on, a babble of agitated wavelets breaking on the rock. Earlier he had actually heard the Squadron Commander instructing his pilots to drop their bombs in the sea.

'*Teniamoci insieme!*' was the order of the day – 'Let's keep together!' The aircraft huddled close and fled for home like frightened hens before a fox. Their aircrews were a startled, indignant bunch of men.

'Didn't expect a welcome, did you?' thought Ciantar. He took off the headphones and put them down on the table. Then he jumped up and went quickly over to the window as he heard the renewed sound of aircraft engines overhead.

Squinting up into the brilliant blue of the Maltese sky he saw what the indignant, frightened Italians had seen a few minutes earlier – he saw the rock their racing waves had broken on.

Down in the narrow, dust-filled street below him, men, women and children had come out from the tall, yellow-walled tenement houses and were staring and pointing upwards into the narrow strip of sky that flowed like a river over their heads. Suddenly three dark shadows fell across the blue stream like bridges, and a heavy roar battered and racketed along the dusty canyon of the street. A young girl with beautiful, ringleted dark hair flung up her brown arm like a wand. Immediately, as if she had tossed a star into the sky, the sun exploded on three bright metallic shapes that flashed like silver fish overhead and then were gone.

'There they are,' she shouted, her dark eyes glowing. 'Faith, Hope and Charity.'

The people of Malta were used to wars. Invasion and conquest were part of their heritage. But this heritage has beauty too, the beauty of a jewel in a lovely setting, a land of ivory and amber couched in the dazzling sea and wind-polished sky of the Mediterranean. Malta is a lovely woman who has been wooed and fought for many times, for her beauty and for the rich dowry that makes her a key to the whole of the ancient sea. Her beauty and her power have woven her history and have moulded the fate of her conquerors, her friends and her lovers. Many nations have sent their sons to Malta, and Malta has set her mark upon them all so that now they either remember her with love or, because they tried to take her by force, with hatred. Many of these lie now in the cockpits of wrecked Macchis and Stukas, under heavy fathoms near that lovely coast, or lend their blood to enrich the loam of Malta's bare, sun-bleached fields.

Many other conquerors have tried to take Malta, long before the Fascists strutted across the Mediterranean stage. As each vortex of power engulfed the Mediterranean world, Malta was swept up by the storm.

The Phoenicians in their hungry voyaging absorbed the island, and they and their offspring, the Carthaginians, held Malta for seven hundred years until Malta, as a dependence of Carthage, became involved in the Punic Wars. With the fall of Carthage, Rome set its heel upon the island. In fact it was in Malta that Hamilcar, son of Gisco, surrendered to the Roman consul Titus Sempronius in 216 BC. A later tyrant, whose pipe-dream was that he was destined to rebuild the

Roman Empire, attempted to make history repeat itself, with less success.

The Roman rule of Malta was, as usual, brassy and brutal. The infamous Verres, having plundered Sicily and sucked it dry, turned to Malta and robbed her of priceless works of art, her beautiful and famous textiles, even of her food – anything and everything that this early Göring could lay his rapacious hand on.

But Roman materialism could not debauch or debase the beauty of Malta. The Greeks had called her 'Melita', 'The island of honey'. The word itself is like a sweet flourish on an antique flute, releasing fawn and nymph from the prison of pines and cypresses and carob trees to soften the yellow fields with a mirage of dancing light as in the haze of a dreamy noonday. A Roman poet saw this beauty. Anna, the beautiful sister of Dido, so Ovid tells us, came to Malta. Flying from Carthage in a slender ship, 'sails taut before the wind', she sailed into the friendly arms of a great harbour and was welcomed by the Maltese.

In later years other swift, slender ships entered the blue waters of Grand Harbour, Valetta, and were welcomed as friends. One of them was a *Dido*, and there was a *Penelope* – the ship her sailors called 'The Pepperpot' because she took so many honourable scars defending beautiful Melita against mutual enemies.

Arabs followed Romans and found a language and culture close to their own behind the bronze mask of Imperial Rome. The Normans came next to Malta and gave place to Angevins, Aragonese and Castilians. These peoples added new customs to the Maltese way of life, new words to their vocabulary. But the basic stock, compounded of Phoenician and Arab, remained. Maltese children are still christened Hannibal today, and there were several Hannibals amongst the Maltese fitters and riggers at Hal Far, Takali and Luqa airfields, who helped to write the latest and most glorious page in Maltese history.

The Arabs held Malta from 870 until the Norman Roger, Count of Sicily, captured the island in 1090. Eventually the little country came under the rule of Ferdinand and Isabella of Castile, who also ruled Sicily, sixty miles away across the water. Sixty miles would mean only a few hours' brisk sailing for the boat from Gozo with the ancient eye of Osiris painted at her bow to ward off evil, and only ten minutes' flying time for the Macchi or Me 109 roaring over her masthead, bent upon nothing but evil.

Malta passed by inheritance to the grandson of Ferdinand and Isabella, the Emperor Charles V. Charles gave the island to the Knights of the Order of St John of Jerusalem, and a splendid phase in Maltese history began.

The Knights moved into the island in 1530 and the Grand Master installed himself in the Fort of St Angelo, on the eastern side of Grand Harbour – in later years HMS *St Angelo*, the British Naval Headquarters.

But the Turks were driving through the Mediterranean against the Christian countries of the west. Suleiman, who had earlier driven the Knights from Rhodes, realised the vital importance of Malta in Mediterranean strategy, rising as it did from the middle of the inland sea, and in 1551 he sent his general Dragut to the area. Dragut raided Malta and sacked the citadel of the neighbouring island of Gozo. In 1565 Suleiman sent him once more to Malta, this time with a huge army and a fleet of 181 sails to capture the island for Islam.

For four bloody, bitter months the Knights and the people of Malta endured the siege. As they bled and starved and suffered, the eyes of the world were upon them. For the Turks were threatening European civilisation and were making a great effort to break out of the Mediterranean and overrun the west. Malta was in the way of this great drive, and Malta had to be eliminated. Otherwise it would be a running wound in the side of the Turkish effort, an ever-threatening mine under their long line of communications stretching the entire length of the Mediterranean.

But the Knights and the Maltese, from the Grand Master La Valette, his Knights and the Maltese nobles down to the ordinary men and women who died in the rubble of broken walls and burned homes, were fiercely determined that the Turks should not take their island. Slowly the defenders were driven back and the numbers of dead mounted. The fate of Christian Europe hung in the balance. La Valette was everywhere, his courage and tenacity inspiring them all, standing coolly in the face of the Turkish cannon, rallying his tired men again and again as walls crumbled and fell before Dragut's horde.

In England they watched the heroic defence with mingled pride and anxiety. The first Queen Elizabeth of England, twenty years before her kingdom withstood and broke the Armada, spoke for the whole of Christian civilisation when she said, 'If the Turks should prevail against the Isle of Malta it is uncertain what further peril might follow to the rest of Christendom.'

The Turks did not prevail. La Valette and his men held them beyond the point of persistence in their bloody and costly struggle. With its general dead and its ranks seriously thinned, the Turkish army withdrew, taking with it the last great hope of Islam for world domination.

The western world breathed again and gave Malta thanks. King Philip of Spain sent the Grand Master a jewelled sword inscribed with the elaborate pun fashionable at the time, 'Plu quam valor valet Valette'.

In the year 1798 Valette's great sword was in Paris and Napoleon Bonaparte was master of Malta. Napoleon had called the Order of St John 'an institution to support in idleness the younger sons of certain privileged families'. This remark has the required revolutionary snarl, but the Order had certainly outlived its purpose. There were many among the Knights and the nobles of Malta who wanted to resist Napoleon, but they were powerless. For the Order was rotten within. There was a fifth column on the island. Many of the younger Knights had absorbed the new revolutionary ideas and had decided that it was time to bring such an aristocratic society as the Order to an end. Foremost among those were many 'collaborationists' amongst the French members of the Order, with the Secretary of the Treasury, Bosredon de Ransijat, as the Quisling of his day. A strong Master might have cured the rot, but the German Von Hompesch was a weakling and totally unable to control the situation. The Maltese, for their part, had never wholly accepted the Knights, who had been thrust upon them originally by a foreign power, to the discomfiture and ignominy of their own nobles. Although the two and a half centuries through which the Order had ruled had raised Malta from a barren island with a few scattered villages to a great centre of culture boasting magnificent palaces, houses and fortifications, the Maltese felt that they owed very little to the Knights, who had, they argued, only fought and built for themselves and the protection of their own.

So the French were invited to take over, and the old order was gone for ever. Malta was a priceless gift for Bonaparte in his designs on Egypt and India, and he lost no time in occupying the island and looting it of its treasures to finance his conquests. He loaded the great three-decker *L'Orient* with gold and silver and jewels.

But *L'Orient*'s treasure never reached the coffers of the Revolution. The British Navy, under Nelson, sank her in Aboukir Bay at the Battle of the Nile. Nelson was much preoccupied with Malta. 'Malta is in our thought, waking and sleeping,' he said. In fact, the Navy was now closely involved in Maltese affairs, and a new alliance was about to come into being.

The harsh treatment given to the Maltese by Napoleon's men set them against the French, and with help from the British squadron under Captain Ball, whom Nelson had set to blockade Malta, they drove the French occupation troops into Valetta. The French were eventually forced to evacuate Malta in 1800, and in 1802 the Treaty of Amiens established an uneasy peace between Britain and France, under the terms of which Malta was to be restored to the Knights of St John, under the protection of Great Britain, France, Austria, Spain and Russia, with a Neapolitan garrison.

The Maltese had played a great part in operations against the French and were totally unsatisfied with the terms of the treaty, feeling that admission to the Order for Maltese Knights was too small a prize for the return of their island to a body that had made no effort to hold it, and for its supervision by an Italian garrison. They had found a new friend and ally and they saw the wisdom of hanging on to him.

Six Maltese deputies went to England, briefed to ask for the incorporation of Malta within the British Empire. But the terms of the treaty had to stand – until, in 1803, Napoleon broke them, and Malta became, more than ever, a priceless jewel in the eyes of French and English. 'Peace or war,' Napoleon said to the British Ambassador in Paris on the eve of hostilities, 'depends upon Malta. I would put you in possession of the Faubourg Saint Antoine rather than of Malta.'

But Britain had kept Governor Ball installed in the Grand Master's Palace in Valetta, although the Grand Master himself had been permitted to come to the island.

In 1815, with Napoleon finally beaten and in exile, the Maltese had their wish. Malta became part of the British Empire and its people 'subjects of the British Crown and entitled to its fullest protection'.

From this time on the British Navy remained a trusted friend of the Maltese people. This friendship was finally cemented in 1869 when the Suez Canal was opened and ships of all nations began to pass through the Mediterranean on their way to the East. Malta now became a watchdog on the great sea-lane linking East with West, a frontier post at the neck of a pass between Occident and Orient which, in the hands of an occupying power, could dominate the whole of that vital route as well as the coasts on either side of it, with their land access to the East.

The immediate result was to turn Malta into a first-class British naval base. The Senior Service became as familiar to the Maltese as the goats in their fields or the priests' hats in the streets. Great ships, battleships and cruisers, sailed in and out of the blue waters of Grand Harbour in the shadow of the palaces and fortifications built by the Knights on either hand of that long tongue of the sea. While the ships were in port the officers played polo and the men disported themselves on crafty runs ashore to the tawdry, garish nightspots of The Gut, or Strait Street as that narrow primrose path of exciting iniquity is properly called. When the Fleet went out on its annual cruise the Maltese enjoyed several weeks of peace.

Year by year through the gentle times of peace this routine of gracious, spacious living went on, with an endless dream of white awnings in the sun and brasswork shining, of delicious, faun-like afternoons on the praetorial estates of Maltese noblemen, of Mimi and Manon at the beautiful Opera House in Kingsway.

One day in 1904 an amusing diversion occurred in the solid round of Edwardian Valetta. You opened your newspaper at the Union Club and read out to your guest, a rather stiff young naval officer, the following paragraph:

'The balloons which recently paid a prolonged visit to Malta found the conditions on the island singularly unconducive to air operations. One of them, the balloon called "Trusty", was found, when unpacked, to have provided sustenance for mice or insects.'

'It'll be aeroplanes next,' you said. And talking of aeroplanes, what does the Navy think about them? What is the conquest of the air going to do to your firm?'

'Very little,' the stiff young man might have replied. 'It's ships and guns that will always win wars, and there's no getting away from that.'

And that, to one young Dartmouth-moulded mind at any rate, was that. But if our young officer could have looked a quarter of a century ahead he might have been considerably astonished to see that day in the year 1929 when he brought his command, a 20,000-ton aircraft carrier, into Grand Harbour, with its squadrons already on the ground at Hal Far aerodrome.

By that year Hal Far had been in use for some time as a shore base for the aircraft from the Mediterranean Fleet carriers, whenever those odd and ugly hybrids were in harbour. There used to be an annual air pageant at the aerodrome, to which Maltese, young and old, flocked, just as people at home in England were coming in droves to see Sir Alan Cobham's Air Circus and paying their ten bob for a flip in an Avro.

The carriers belonged to the Navy, which was part of the Maltese landscape, but the aircraft were flown mainly by men from the baby of the three Services, the Royal Air Force, a youngster only just over ten years old. They had no permanent shore base. The only aeroplanes to drone through the clear skies over Malta were the ungainly Fairey Flycatchers from the ships.

But in 1929 the old order changed. Hal Far was officially opened as a Royal Air Force Station. A Station Flight was created and remained in occupation there until 1935, its Fairey 3F aircraft being augmented from time to time by the Flycatchers of 802, 812, 823 and 825 Squadrons from the carriers.

The Abyssinian crisis caused great activity at Hal Far. All Fleet Air Arm squadrons embarked in a hurry, their pilots all with high hopes of a scrap with Mussolini's new 'Eagles of the Air', who were adept at bombing unarmed natives but who might not relish having their elegant trousers removed by The Branch. Two squadrons of Hawker Demons and a Coastal Defence Development Flight of two Wildebeest aircraft came out to take their place.

The crisis passed. Mussolini was appeased, and the Demons and Wildebeests went back to England, like ungainly swallows to an uneasy summer. The Fleet Air Arm squadrons returned unsatisfied to Malta. The thunder had been heard in the distance, however, and many felt that the real storm would not be long in coming.

But still the loveliness of sea and sky and sunlight cradled the Island of Honey and rocked it to sleep. Like everyone else in the torpid, though uneasy western world, the people of Malta, British and Maltese alike, were blind to the beauty that lay around them and in front of their eyes. With them the good things of peace went unsung and unappreciated. Soon it would be too late. The beauty of palace and villa, of green garden and lazy blue water, went for nothing with people who had grown used to the luxury of a place in the sun. Soon that lovely landscape would be darkened and there would be only the bittersweet memory of it left.

Only an airman might have seen the beauty of this island clear and whole, suddenly sighting her, sun focusing through the bright lens of his eye. Then it would be, as with John Pudney's airman,

> 'Look! Malta spun on the sea, shaping to sight
> Fragilely as a promise, framed by metal
> And the deft handling of airmanship.
> Nudge. Nod. That's there all right. A petal
> Yellow, all veined with green in the sea's hard
> Flooring of other element, of timeless running.
> Malta, upon the blood-invested water, cactus, nettle-
> Leafed, old prickle, guard.'

'Cactus … old prickle, guard', and a jewel too, a chameleon, whose colours glittered and changed in the harsh sunlight, an island nibbled and gnawed by the sea into honey-coloured cliffs and bays of amber rock set with translucent emerald.

Around the island, and its little neighbour Gozo to the north, the Mediterranean, shimmering and still under the sun, catching his rays like an immense glass and throwing their splinters of light into the eye. And the airman, in his ivory tower of the air, were he a British pilot on a training flight or an Italian bringing the Alittoria flying boat in on his daily trip, would idly watch the shadow of his wings in the mirror of the water, and think how small the island was, and how fragile.

He would see an island by nature barren and rocky, of limestone and yellow sandstone, not much more than a rock itself in the middle of the sea, a rock only seventeen miles by nine, where a network of rough stone walls protected its thin soil from the *gregale*, the 'Greek Wind' that shipwrecked St Paul upon this coast, the destroying wind that sweeps across it from the open sea. He would see a place where grass is a fine, rare luxury, where wheat, vine, olive, orange and lemon must be wrested from the earth. Bare, sun-bleached, by nature barren and un-fruitful, carved out of tawny rock, but a beautiful island. It was here that the nymph Calypso enchanted Ulysses, promising the hero immortal life if he would make it his home for ever.

Bathed in Mediterranean light, then, the island lies before him, glowing and still in the sun, beautiful and fragile. Lazily, in a haze of jazzing light, the long waves advance on a shore that seems such an easy target for a bomb.

He is nearer now, over the capital city Valetta. He can see twin harbours, magnificent for ships, divided by a promontory. On that promontory Valetta, the town of La Valette, itself, with a fort at the tip of it, St Elmo, where a handful of Christian knights and Maltese men and women once died to save Malta and the western world from slavery. Yes, a jewel, this city, amethyst in a setting of ivory and pearl, where the blue water reflects the undulating shadows of white palaces and churches rising in tiers of gracious, exquisitely wrought stone. If the airman were British he might feel vaguely disturbed at the thought that war might come soon to this pleasant place and he might wonder dimly when the balloon would go up. If he were Italian, bringing in his flying boat to Marsa Scirocco Bay on the south of the island, then he too might regret that his beautiful birdman's view might soon be lost – unless, of course, the Maltese would see reason. For, as the Duce said, were not the Maltese and the Italians brothers? If he was fond of Malta he might wish that her people *would* see reason. Otherwise... He might shake his head sadly at the picture of all that loveliness below lying in blackened ruins. For he had inside knowledge of just when the balloon was likely to go up.

One day, as the Italian flying boat circled round, preparing to touch down on the peaceful water, a sergeant from the Royal Air Force Aircraft Repair Section at Kalafrana squinted upwards into the sun.

'There's the Eyetie kite now,' he said to his mate, who stopped wiping his hands on a bit of oily rag and looked up.

'Come to do a bit more snooping for Mussolini,' he said.

'You said it,' said the sergeant. He pointed up at the flying boat. 'They'll keep that bloody thing going till the last minute before the shooting starts, you see, to see whether we move in any more stuff – not,' the sergeant paused gloomily, 'not that there's a snowball's chance in hell of that! He can see everything we've got, the whole layout. And Hal Far only just up the road!'

'Not much to see there now anyway,' said the other man, adding his mite to the gloom. 'Two Maggies and a couple of bloody Stringbags that Noah wouldn't have in the flaming Ark! What happens when the Regia-bloody-Aeronautica comes over? We get caught with our pants down – as per usual!'

'If the Eyeties come we've had our flipping lot, don't make any mistake about that,' said the sergeant. 'Hal Far'll cop it for a start. *Then* what've we got? Damn all! Can you speak Eyetie?'

'No, sarge.'

'Well, you'd better ruddy well learn.'

'But aren't they doing anything about it? Don't they know we got sweet fanny on the island?'

'Well, if *I* knew the answer I'd be the AO ruddy C instead of a flaming time-expired, browned-off sergeant. And I don't suppose the AOC knows any better than I do. He has to take what they send him. Come on, let's get weaving. I'm getting browned off with watching that macaroni-chewing bastard going round in circles.'

The 'answer', did they but know it, lay right behind them, about twelve inches from their backs. In fact the sergeant had leaned on it as he prognosticated so bitterly.

The answer lay inside several large packing cases marked 'Royal Naval Stores'. They stood waiting for shipment there on the slipway, only, like the three old ladies in the rugby song, nobody knew they were there.

CHAPTER TWO

Waiting for War

Two men – one Maltese the other Italian – were talking in the back room of a quiet bar in Valetta. Outside in Kingsway, the main thoroughfare of Valetta, men and women were thronging to and fro, up and down the long street stretching from the Royal Opera House at the higher end down to the Royal Palace at the other, where Kingsway becomes a narrow alley declining abruptly in the harbour.

It was sunset time, Malta's enchanted hour. The walls of houses rising from the narrow streets glowed golden in the light of the westering sun. The last rays glimmered on the sea, silky with purple light. The yellow rocks shone fitfully like gold indications in a pile of stone. Then the sun disappeared and the light died from the sea like the rainbow from a silver fish as the island took on the velvet softness of dusk.

Outside, young lovers giggled and clasped their hot hands nervously together. Countrywomen in sombre black passed like shadows. The black faldettas shrouding their heads and faces filled with the cool evening breeze that sighed through the streets, so that they looked like yachts running lightly before the wind, their black spinnakers stretched tight with the following breeze.

In the bar it was cool and quiet. But the Maltese looked hot and uncomfortable. His forehead was moist and he stared into space, biting his lip. The two men spoke in whispers, for what they had to say would not be popular.

'You may be right,' said the Maltese, looking nervously about him. It was to be noticed that his Italian was as fluent as his friend's.

'Of course I'm right.' The Italian leaned forward, his eyes intent upon the other's face, as if trying to hypnotise him. 'Look at the situation practically. For over a hundred years

Malta has lived under the heel of a foreign power, her own people slighted and snubbed, treated like ignorant colonials by the white Raj, slaves to British interests. I tell you British Imperialism has bled you white, Malta is Cunningham's lackey.' He paused for a second and his voice became urgent, dramatic. 'It is time that you threw off your chains.'

'But the British are not as bad as that. They are our friends, we are part of the British Empire,' protested the Maltese.

'The British Empire no longer exists. It is effete and rotten, ready to fall apart. It could no longer help you or protect you, even if it wanted to. *And it does not want to.* Believe me,' his eyes flashed eloquently, 'believe me, Great Britain is great no longer. She is a second-rate power, she no longer cares for her precious family of imperial scapegoats. Chamberlain – an old woman with an umbrella! Now the Duce...' Once again he paused dramatically, so that the blue-jowled, strutting figure seemed to materialise like a genie before them. 'The Duce has your interests at heart. You know that as well as I do, you have lived in Italy. Over and over again he has said that the Maltese and the Italians are brothers. What have you in common with the British? Nothing. They are the masters and you are their slaves. But we Italians are your own kind. We are of the same family, and we should stick together like all families. Soon the time will come when the Maltese will have to choose between their conquerors and their brothers. At the strategic hour we shall strike at the British and drive them forever from Our Sea. Our navy is ready and eager, cruisers and battleships are waiting now with steam up in Taranto to sail out and smash the miserable handful of British ships that still lord it over an Italian lake. Above all, our glorious air force is all-powerful. Our young eagles are burning to do what Roman eagles have done before – to spread the new Roman Empire throughout the world! One taste of our bombs and the British will desert you, they will leave Malta to her fate. They have already planned to abandon you.'

He leaned forward, ready with his masterstroke to say the last word in an argument that was, to him, merely a repetition of the obvious.

'Why else do you think they have left you without the protection of fighters?'

That the Maltese might have felt his reason weakening under the bombast of such a tirade would have been less a tribute to the logic of Fascist argument than a compliment to the effectiveness of the Italian propaganda, which had for years been working upon the Maltese mind with spurious arguments 'proving' that Malta was linked racially with the people of Italy, that Maltese and Italians were, in fact, blood brothers. Their evidence was spurious but their job was made easier by the presence of some Italian sympathisers among the Maltese.

Much was made of the fact that both the Maltese language and the Sicilian dialect contained a large number of Arabic words. The Fascists argued that both were dialects of Italian. It was true that Maltese contained many Italian words. But it had also absorbed many Spanish, French and English words, to quote but a few examples of how a basically Oriental language, thoroughly Semitic in structure, had reflected the occupation of so many foreign powers. But a few Maltese believed what Mussolini told them. To them Malta was pictured as an Italian colony under the corrupt and vicious power of the degenerate British.

The naked truth, behind all the slimy Fascist tricks, was that Mussolini was bent on conquering the Mediterranean and converting it into an 'Italian lake', and, like Suleiman and Napoleon before him, he had to have Malta to do it. Malta was an outpost, a fortress rising from the sea between Europe and Africa. The island lay in a direct line between Sicily – only sixty miles away to the north – and Tripoli, the only good port in Mussolini's African colony.

A beautiful island, a military strongpoint. If he could not get it by propaganda he would take it by force. As a target for his invincible air force it would be only too pathetically easy.

He looked at his map. Printed across it in huge letters were the words '*Mare 'Nostrum*', 'Our Sea'. To make these words mean anything he must conquer all the Mediterranean seaboard and, above all, drive the British out of Egypt. And one miserable little island was in the way, an island that could be used as a refuge for British ships and a base for air and sea attacks on his ports and on convoys supplying his African army.

One little island. *Eliminate it*.

Britain knew what was in the Italian dictator's mind and knew too that she must prevent Malta from falling into Italian hands, to be turned against us in the event of a war. British policy was to hold Malta at all costs. Malta and her people must be protected and the safety of the British Empire, of which Malta was a part, safe-guarded. At the same time Britain itself must, if war came, do what Mussolini most feared – use Malta as a base from which it could hit the enemy with bomb, mine and torpedo.

Meanwhile the Italians rehearsed for the great day when Italian arms began their drive to conquer the world. In Abyssinia, Bruno Mussolini, the artist, experimented with the use of bombs, fascinated, as he said, by the beautiful patterns made by exploding bombs in the midst of natives armed with bows and arrows and spears. Later the Fascists, and their brave brothers in arms the Nazis, continued their 'manoeuvres' against women and children in the open cities of Spain. It was all good, honest, manly fun, fit exercise and battle practice for the heroes of totalitarianism.

Munich came and went. Once more Mussolini saw clear evidence of the weakness and decadence of Britain. Then Hitler marched into Prague and tore up the Munich agreement. A week later he bullied Lithuania into handing over Memelland.

This was Mussolini's cue, and on 7 April 1939 he invaded Albania. The eagles had marched. Then Hitler turned his hysterical wrath on Poland. Britain and France pledged themselves to support her in the event of an open attack by

Germany. Gradually things went from bad to worse until war was seen to be inevitable.

On 3 September it came. But Mussolini held his hand. He wanted to be sure.

On the outbreak of war Britain and France divided the responsibility for the defence of the Mediterranean between them. A British destroyer force was set to guard the Straits of Gibraltar, while the French Navy, with bases at Bizerta, Algiers and Oran, undertook to hold the western Mediterranean between Malta and Gibraltar. The main British Fleet waited and watched at Alexandria, guarding the eastern basin, Egypt and the Middle East, ready for action, though careful not to force the issue by any flaunting of arms within sight of Italian shores.

It was a strong position and Mussolini took heed of it. He announced a policy of non-belligerency, limited the extent of Italian submarine patrols, and kept his large, modern fleet swinging at anchor.

Tension relaxed at once. Normal trade routes, closed immediately at the outbreak of war, were reopened and ships sailed through on their peaceful business. Once more merchantmen steamed in and out of Grand Harbour in the deep, saffron shadows of the old forts. The only concession to war conditions was that they had to run in convoys, with destroyer escorts to protect them against possible attacks from German submarines. But the U-boats were busy elsewhere, saving their torpedoes for the *Athenia* and other unfortunate vessels who exposed themselves on the wide and naked Atlantic.

As in the North Atlantic, the Navy established a rigid system of contraband control in the eastern Mediterranean. British warships patrolled the Aegean, the approaches to the Adriatic, and the waters to the south of the Straits of Messina. A contraband control base was set up in Malta and ships suspected of carrying cargoes ultimately destined for Germany were sent there or to Port Said or Haifa under escort. The Navy stood sentry at Gibraltar and Suez, sealing off the whole Mediterranean from the enemy.

So effectively did they do this that no German submarines got through into the Mediterranean. The convoy system was abandoned and ships proceeded without escort. It was the period of the 'phoney war'.

In Malta life was, if anything, too peaceful. The Fleet had left the Mediterranean for better hunting grounds and the resulting vacuum was felt to be highly artificial and unnatural. Under the smiling surface Malta's nerves were a little strained. *Dghaissas*, bright boats like gondolas, glided across the harbour between Valetta and the Three Cities district, composed of the old mediaeval 'cities' of Senglea, Vittoriosa and Cospicua, famous in the time of the Knights and now grouped around the naval barracks and dockyards on that side of the harbour. Carozzin carriages clopped and jingled through the streets. People still went to the opera and wept over the high tragedies of fiction. In Strait Street the tawdry fairyland of the dives and cabarets glittered and screeched its jaded welcome, although there was not much business now that the Fleet had gone. All along the waterfront the lights of bars and cafés cast spears of blood-red light into the dark water. Malta was still at peace.

Admiral Cunningham was now a Commander-in-Chief without a fleet. He moved from Alexandria to Malta in November and hoisted his flag there. He made use of the period of peace to cement professional and personal relationships with the Commanding Officers and staffs of the Allied navies in the Mediterranean. Frequent conferences were held where plans were made against the need for concerted action in the future, for no one knew quite what sort of a game Mussolini was playing or when and if he would strike. All these meetings were successful. An atmosphere of close friendship and harmony of thought and resolution prevailed, which gave every promise of success should the need to combine against the Italian Navy arise.

In addition, Admiral Cunningham visited Allied army and air force commands in North Africa and Syria.

The small British army in Egypt was reinforced by Australian and New Zealand contingents, which went into training for possible operations against an Italian army striking east from Libya down the new Italian motor road linking Bardia, Tobruk, Derna and Benghazi along the North African coast. All the time a continuous reinforcement of the Italian army in Africa went on. Italian troopships steamed across to Tripoli within easy aircraft range of Malta.

But there were no aircraft in Malta, except the obsolete handful comprising the Station Flight at Hal Far. Even the four 'London' flying boats of 202 Squadron had left for Gibraltar at the end of 1939. In its determination to hold Malta at all costs Britain put its trust in France, looking to French aircraft, from their powerful air and naval base at Bizerta, to defend Malta and counter the threat of Italian air raids on the island by the obvious fact that French bombers could raid Italian cities in reprisal. It was thought that the threat would be sufficient to deter the Italians. Nevertheless four fighter squadrons were to be sent to Malta as soon as they became available.

In November 1939, just after Admiral Cunningham had hoisted his flag in Malta, the new Air Officer Commanding Royal Air Force Mediterranean arrived. He was Air Commodore F. H. M. Maynard AFC, a New Zealand officer serving with the RAF. Air Commodore Maynard had flown in the Great War, having joined the Royal Naval Air Service in 1915. To this experience of wartime air fighting he could add varied and distinguished service between the wars, including two tours of duty in the Middle East and various commands in the organisation of the air defence of Great Britain. Now he came straight to Malta from the Air Ministry with the overall task of looking after the air defence at this far smaller, far more vulnerable island. Besides being a distinguished and experienced officer, the new AOC was in everything a gentleman, a quiet, able, thorough and determined man with none of the flashy trappings and film-star swagger of many high-ranking officers determined to blaze a meteoric career for themselves across the dark sky of war. Maynard preferred application to applause. He came to Malta and quietly went to work to marshal his slender resources and do whatever lay in his power to prepare the island as an effective air base, both in defence and attack.

As soon as Maynard arrived in Malta, Admiral Cunningham invited him to stay with him, and the AOC lived at Admiralty House for six weeks. Together the C-in-C and the AOC Mediterranean went over the problems of defending Malta and thrashed out ideas and plans for the future. Thus the cooperation of the RAF and the Navy, which would be so vital in action, got off to a good start. The cordial relations established at Admiralty House between the two officers were to bear fruit in a way nobody could then foresee. One thing they must both have wished for above all was the establishment of a fighter defence force, but they did not look like getting one. Many times they aired the problem but it could only end in frustration. 'When the war started we were at the mercy of Italian bombers,' Admiral Cunningham said later, looking back on the gloomy situation in those days.

All they could do was to hope and wait on events, both looking forward to the time when those precious fighter squadrons would arrive. True, the Mediterranean was at peace and Italy was a declared non-belligerent, but the word of the Fascist dictator was cheap and both officers foresaw a time when things might not be so peaceful, when Malta would be crying out for aircraft to defend her.

As 1939 passed into 1940 events began to show that this time might not be far off. In April Hitler brought the 'phoney war' abruptly to an end by invading Denmark and Norway. Denmark fell at once but Norway resisted, crippled though she was by the activities of a powerful fifth column under the notorious Quisling.

The British Army and Navy fought desperately alongside the Norwegian forces but slowly they were pushed back by weight of numbers and immensely superior air power.

German Stuka dive-bombers in particular did great execution, as potential targets of Axis bombs were quick to notice. The dive-bombers smashed continuously at Britain's ships and men and knocked out its small air effort. In no time at all the Luftwaffe had a force of four hundred bombers in the air, a force that increased rapidly, hour by hour, and piled on the pressure, sinking Allied ships and savaging unprotected armies. Once again the totalitarian powers demonstrated the effectiveness of *blitzkrieg* from the air.

No 263 Squadron of Gloster Gladiators and No 46 Squadron of Hawker Hurricanes had been landed in Norway from *Furious* and *Glorious*, and these few fought magnificently with heavy losses until the survivors were finally evacuated by *Glorious*. The Hurricane pilots flew their aircraft aboard the carrier without accident in spite of the fact that none of them had ever deck-landed before and their aircraft were not equipped for the job. It was a tragic reward for their gallantry when *Glorious* was sunk on the way back to Scapa Flow.

On 31 April the last British and Allied forces were evacuated from Norway and the whole country, with its long seaboard facing the east coast of Britain, fell into German hands.

With the fall of Norway came the collapse of the Chamberlain government, and Winston Churchill took over the direction of British affairs. Within a few days of his taking office the Nazis invaded Holland and Belgium.

By now Italy had begun to change her attitude from one of neutrality to a sullen, but so far passive, hostility. As the Nazi *blitzkrieg* went from success to success, Mussolini finally took heart. The capture of Norway gave him a final shove and made the young eagles of his air force strain at the leash, burning to emulate the successes of the Luftwaffe. The signs were all too obvious and the British Battle Fleet moved back into the Mediterranean, to be reinforced there by cruisers from the East Indies Station, submarines from China, and the aircraft carrier *Eagle*.

In Malta the atmosphere had become very tense and the worst was expected at any moment. It was obvious to Air Commodore Maynard that he could forget all about those four fighter squadrons, at least for some time. They were going to be all too desperately needed in the West.

For France was fighting desperately for her life and the Allied armies were breaking under the weight of the German *blitzkrieg*.

Once more Mussolini looked at his map. This time he was encouraged and heartened by what he saw. France and Britain were being beaten and crushed in the west. The Mediterranean had been closed and all supplies and reinforcements for the British Army in Egypt would have to come round the Cape, taking two or three months to reach Egypt. The Italian Air Force, concentrated strategically all over the Mediterranean, far outnumbered Allied air strength in the area. Mussolini's powerful navy, too, was far larger than Britain's Mediterranean Fleet.

Just sixty miles away from Malta, in Sicily, were the airfields of the Regia Aeronautica. There, bombers and fast fighters lay in readiness to take off against their 'blood brothers', ten minutes' flying time away to the south. Not that fighters would be needed. There was no opposition.

The Fascist Air Force was sleek, fat and confident. The Italian air crews were the favoured sons, forming the shining spearhead of Mussolini's legions. The dictator himself, as Secretary for Air, exercised direct control over his eagles. As a keen pilot himself, whether from enthusiasm or expediency, and a lover of athletics and their 'strength through joy', he was an inspiration to his young winged athletes. They did not hear the young, anti-Fascist airman-poet Lauro de Bossis when he reminded them of the fate of Icarus. They only had eyes for the sunlit mirage that was Fascism and for their perverter and betrayer Mussolini. The sun that shone into their uplifted, dedicated eyes and glittered on the metallic sheen of their own Italian sea could never melt *their* wings, for they were invincible.

And so far there had been nothing to prove them misguided. The Regia Aeronautica had been the only competitor to challenge British supremacy in the final Schneider Trophy competitions. Its machines had captured the world's altitude record, held several long-distance records, and had made three record-breaking formation flights across the North and South Atlantic.

They had been 'blooded' in war, too. With the memory of their glorious victories against unarmed men, women and children in Abyssinia still fresh, the new legions of the skies were ready and eager to conquer the world for Fascism, convinced that the victory would be swift and easy.

Ringing in their proud young minds were the words of men like Guilio Douhet, the prophet and high priest of strategic bombing. Douhet, the Mahan of air warfare, a figure held in international respect for his theories, had said,

> 'The air arm is the arm, not of a rich people, but of a young people, ardent, bold, inventive, who love space and height. It is, therefore, an arm eminently suited to us Italians. The importance it has attained and its influence on the general character of war are favourable to us; it is the arm best suited to the genius of our race; and surely the solid organisation and strong discipline which bind the Italian people in unity is the most adequate force to give us courage to face the terrible effects which would come from an aerial war, even if victorious.'

Was Douhet nerving the Italian people against reprisal raids by French bombers? He went on,

> 'Our geographical position, which serves us as a bridge across the Mediterranean, makes the air arm still more vital to us.'

Then came the operative clause. In ringing words of brass he thus handed the torch of destiny to his young aircrews:

> 'Visualise Rome as the centre of a zone with a radius

of 1,000 kilometres, normal range for a plane today, and you will find within the circumference the whole of the ancient Roman Empire.

To dominate our own sky will mean to dominate the Mediterranean sky. Let us therefore look to the future with hope and confidence and give thanks to all those whose daring and ingenuity have made this arm powerful.'

From this yawning 'space and height' of an 'Italian' sky that called to them from beyond the horizons of 'the ancient Roman Empire', echelons of bombers, patterned in meticulous formation, would deliver their bombs. One raid would be enough.

'The guiding principles of bombing actions should be this: the objective must be destroyed completely in one attack, making further attack on the same target unnecessary.'

And if, by some unaccountable mischance, it should not be enough...

'A people who are bombed today as they were bombed yesterday, who know they will be bombed again tomorrow and see no end to their martyrdom, are bound to call for peace at length.'

Sixty miles away Malta watched, and waited.

People in the streets stopped and looked up, half expecting to see Italian bombers in the sky. Radios were kept on all day for news of Mussolini's intentions. But the jackal waited until his victim seemed helpless before he struck. On 10 June he finally decided that France and Britain were beaten nations.

Kingsway is always crowded in the evening. There the whole city of Valetta seems to promenade, laughing and chattering. The street is narrow and the walls enclosing it are high, so the babble of voices is magnified into a great torrent of sound.

So it was on the night of 10 June 1940. Suddenly a new cry started and passed rapidly from mouth to mouth.

'*Guerra ... Mussolini iddikjara guerra...*'

'War ... Mussolini has declared war...'

And from the Palazzo Venezia, Mussolini was speaking to the Italian people. When the cheering had died and the hysterical thousands had stopped baying their wave upon wave of '*Duce ... Duce ... Duce*', the new Caesar struck his blue-jowled chin forward and shouted,

'Fighters of the land, the sea and the air, Blackshirts of the revolution and of the legions, men and women of Italy, of the Empire and the other kingdom of Albania, listen. The hour marked out by destiny is sounding in the sky of our country. This is the hour of irrevocable decisions. The declaration of war has already been handed to the ambassadors of Britain and France!'

At this point the cheering broke out anew and rose to a fanatical roar as the hypnotised Romans threw up their right arms in worship of the dire figure on the balcony. Mussolini put up his hand for silence, his heavy, pork-butcher's face stern, his eyes glowing. He began again.

'We are going to war against the plutocratic and reactionary democracies of the West, who have hindered the advance and often threatened the existence of the Italian people. The events of quite recent history can be summarised in these words: half-promises, constant threats, blackmail and, finally, as the crown of this ignoble edifice...'

And while Mussolini fulminated in his balcony, the Lieutenant-Governor of Malta, Sir William Dobbie, spoke quietly to his people. He said:

'The decision of His Majesty's Government to fight until our enemies are defeated will be heard with the greatest satisfaction by all ranks of the garrison of

Malta. It may be that hard times lie ahead of us, but I know that however hard they may be, the courage and determination of all ranks will not falter, and that with God's help we will maintain the security of this fortress. I call on all officers and men humbly to seek God's help, and then in reliance on Him to do their duty unflinchingly.'

Gradually the crowds left the streets and the noise of their chatter died away. The last carozzins carried their loads of excited, apprehensive people home. Silence crept slowly out of the darkness and settled on the island.

In Kingsway, only the clanging of the street cleaner's shovel, the solitary footstep, remained to break the silence, the last 'good night' echoing wistfully down the unfamiliar wasteland of the blacked-out street. The last shops put up their shutters, the last waiters went home, the last dog howled in a side alley. A cold wind swept over the island, as its people slept in the limbo between peace and war.

Slowly the night hours dragged through with no alarms. The early dawn crept up on Malta from the sea, grey and weary. Men woke, yawned, then got up and went to the window to look anxiously out at the sky. Perhaps it was just a bad dream after all. The people began their normal daily round. In fact, the day still had sleep in its eyes when the sirens howled.

The Italians had timed their first raid well. They had picked the hour of the day when people had just come into the streets or were beginning their work, their minds and bodies heavy and uneasy with sleep and half-remembered nightmares, psychologically at their worst to withstand the terror effects of bombing.

For the Italians everything went according to plan. As they approached Valetta, they split up into two formations, one making for Hal Far, the other for the naval dockyard. They dropped their bombs, turned, formed up again and headed back towards Sicily. They had seen no trace of any British aircraft, nor had they expected any.

A gunner in the starboard rear aircraft sang softly to himself.

'*Vido mare quante bello…*' He smiled. How appropriate. The sea did look beautiful in the early morning light, hushed and still. He wondered what it would look like when they came back in half an hour's time. The sun would be up by then, bathing them in warm light as they brought their second load of death to Malta.

'*Vido mare quante bello,*
Spira tantu sentimente…'

And that was as far as he got with his serenade. For, just beneath him, a row of bullet holes had appeared in the fuselage and his song was drowned by the clatter of machine-guns.

There was a fighter on their tail.

CHAPTER THREE

Gift Horses

By the end of March it had become obvious to Air Commodore Maynard that he would not be able to count on the four precious fighter squadrons that had been earmarked for Malta. Home squadrons would have top priority. There would be no Hawker Hurricanes at Hal Far or Takali or the new airfield at Luqa for many months to come.

But something had to be done.

There was still the French Air Force in Tunisia, but that hardly answered the urgent need for fighters that could intercept raids over Malta itself at very short notice. British commanders have been faced only too often with the job of making a little go a long way. But the AOC had nothing whatever, save a few non-operational aircraft.

Then one day his Chief Administrative Officer, Group Captain N. G. Gardner, told him that there were some Sea-Gladiator aircraft belonging to the Navy in packing cases on the slipway at the Aircraft Repair Section at Kalafrana. These aircraft were the first-line reserve for the fighter squadron in the *Glorious* but had missed the carrier when she had sailed a few weeks earlier on her way to take part in the Norwegian campaign. Had the Malta Gladiators gone with her when they should have done they might have met their end on the frozen surface of Lake Lesja or in the waters of the North Sea when *Glorious* was sunk in the evacuation of Norway.

But they were in Malta. And they were fighters. Could the RAF get permission to take them over from their naval owners? Maynard and Gardner went over the problems involved. They decided that if they could have some of the aircraft they could detach enough maintenance personnel to look after them and find pilots to fly them from the few then on the island.

There were eight Gladiators altogether. Admiral Cunningham and his staff had thought that the fighters could probably be used in the *Eagle*, which was about to join the Mediterranean Fleet. The *Eagle* had no fighter squadron and was not fitted in any way for operating fighters, but nevertheless they thought that she could probably handle them.

Then the AOC came to see the Chief of Naval Staff, Rear-Admiral Willis, and asked him if he could have the aircraft, or some of them, to form a fighter force for the defence of Malta. The C-in-C and his staff talked over the idea and it was agreed that Maynard could have four of the Gladiators. They would put the other four in the *Eagle* when she came out and hope that she would be able to operate them. The matter was urgent and there was no time to ask for Admiralty permission. The Admiralty was informed later as a matter of routine on a 'disposal of aircraft' signal. The Governor was informed of the transfer and the job of unpacking and erecting the four machines was begun.

The aircraft themselves, though obsolescent, were of a type that had already proved its worth in air combat. Both the Royal Air Force and the Fleet Air Arm had been equipped with them.

The Gladiators were the last of the biplane fighters. They were the descendants of the Pups, Camels and SE 5As used by the RFC, the RNAS, and later the newly created RAF, in the First World War. Their own particular family tree was a complex and distinguished one. The Gloster Gladiator was one of the most successful and illustrious names in a long line of machines designed by Mr H. P. Folland. Its immediate ancestors were the Gauntlet, and its prototypes the SS 19b, the SS 19, the SS 18b and the SS 18, a line of development that arose from Air Ministry Specification F20/27. In 1934 the CT37 was produced by the Gloster Company to meet the requirements of Specification F7/30. This was the prototype Gladiator, No K5200. The prototype machine lacked some of the more modern refinements that were to be incorporated in the production model. It had the old Gauntlet-type cowling and 'spitted' tailwheel and did not have the cockpit hood fitted to later machines. But it did possess some modern and outstanding features. The undercarriage was of a new type. It employed Dowty internally sprung streamlined wheels, and the old cumbersome 'birdcage' of struts and bracing wires had been done away with in favour of two graceful, knife-like single legs inside which the 6-inch travel of the Dowty gear absorbed all shocks.

The first delivery of Gladiators was made to the RAF in 1937 under the new Expansion Scheme. The first squadrons to have them were Nos 3, 56 and 72. They soon found that Gloster, the firm that was to produce the Meteor and the Javelin, had given them a winner. The little single-bay biplane was robust and highly manoeuvrable, so that it was exceptionally good for aerobatics. The aircraft seemed to have no faults. Soon, more squadrons received the new machines: Nos 17, 33, 54, 65, 73, 80, 87, 223, 247, 602 (City of Glasgow Squadron), 603 (City of Edinburgh Squadron), 607 (County of Durham Squadron) and 615 (County of Surrey Squadron). The Gladiator continued to show herself a star performer in the aerobatic line. In 1938 at the RAF Air Show three of them flew chained together in V formation. In 1939 the naval version of the Gladiator, called the Sea-Gladiator, was introduced into the Fleet Air Arm. This version of the machine incorporated various special naval fittings, including a deck-arrester hook, a dinghy and several internal modifications.

All these machines were Mark I Gladiators, which had the Bristol Mercury Mark 9 engine, another guarantee of quality performance. The Mark 9 drove a fixed-pitch, two-bladed, wooden propeller. Later the Mark II was introduced, powered by the 810-horsepower Mercury 8A. At the outbreak of war many of these were in service, large numbers of them fitted with three-bladed, fixed-pitch Fairey Reed-type metal propellers. The variable-pitch propeller was an innovation that had not reached them.

The Gloster Gladiator was basically of all-metal

construction, of steel tube and strip. The fuselage was of the Warren girder type with steel tubes and internal wire bracing. The wings were based upon two spars made of steel strip with steel compression ribs and dural lattice ribs. The whole aircraft was fabric-covered. The internal structure made for great strength and durability. Little did the men who had planned and built the aircraft know what a severe test this same structure would one day be put to.

Armament consisted of four .303 machine-guns, two of them in the fuselage, firing forward between the propeller blades by means of an interrupter gear, and two in 'blisters' under the wings. The aircraft had a maximum speed of 250mph at 15,500 feet, could climb to 15,000 feet in 5.8 minutes and reached its ceiling at 32,800 feet. It cruised at 210mph and landed at 59mph. A main tank and a gravity tank had a fuel capacity of 64 gallons and 20 gallons respectively.

The Gladiator was the last biplane to be constructed by the Gloster Company and the last biplane to be operationally employed by the RAF. A total of 527 were built altogether and, of these, a total of 216 were supplied to the governments of Belgium, China, Greece, Finland, Iraq, the Irish Free State, Latvia, Lithuania, Portugal, Norway and Sweden.

By the time war came, the Gladiator was on its way out, and most front-line squadrons of the RAF had been re-equipped with Hurricanes. The Gladiator, with its mixture of ancient and modern features, was something of a transition type. But it was not a mongrel. What it lacked in speed and armament it made up for a great deal in manoeuvrability, reliability and sheer airworthiness. It was in fact a pedigree machine, the final flower of the old, sturdy, dog-fighting biplane fighters.

As such it was destined to uphold with great honour the name of the old Air Force. The Gladiator, so aptly named, was to carry the reputation that the old Royal Flying Corps gained against the German Air Force in the First World War into a second Great War, a war in which speeds had trebled, and give it greater glory.

From the very beginning of the war the Gladiators were in the thick of the fight. Nos 607 and 617 Squadrons took their Gladiators to France, where they distinguished themselves. A Gladiator from 603 Squadron scored one of the first air victories of the war by shooting down a Heinkel III into the Firth of Forth.

This was the aircraft that the Air Force hoped to use to defend Malta in the event of an attack by the Regia Aeronautica – a tough, intensively airworthy little aeroplane, but sadly outdated by the modern machines of the Italians. And there were only four of them. What is more, they were Sea-Gladiators, with their deck-landing hooks and other heavy fittings, all of which helped to reduce their already slow speed even further. And there were no spares of any kind.

But the RAF did not make the mistake of looking these gift horses in the mouth. They set about putting them into the air.

The Royal Air Force Station, Kalafrana, was situated on a large bay at the southern end of the island. The station consisted of a flying-boat base with large workshops and stores capable of the repair and maintenance of all aircraft, marine craft and mechanical transport belonging to the RAF on Malta. There was no airfield at Kalafrana, but a specially widened road, a mile in length, connected one entrance of Kalafrana with the airfield at Hal Far. Any other than waterborne aircraft were towed along this road, with their wings either folded or detached.

The Officer-in-Charge of the Aircraft Repair Section at Kalafrana was Flying Officer G. A. V. Collins. He had come to the island in 1936 as a Warrant Officer and had at once thrown himself into the job of bringing the workshops that were his province to the very high standard of efficiency upon which he always insisted. He was a man who believed that a job once begun should be done well. He demanded this of himself and saw that those under his command followed his example. It was normal practice in Malta at that time to work during the morning and 'stand easy' during the afternoon. Collins could never get used to this routine and used to work a full day, afternoon as well. His men must have called him a slave-driver at first, but they soon found out that he only drove them hard because it was necessary, and that he himself worked hardest of all. Besides that, he so obviously knew his job that he gained the respect of his men and the whole-hearted trust and confidence of his superior officers.

And he had another reason for working hard. Collins had seen action before. He had fought through the Great War as a soldier, an infantryman, before he joined the RAF, and he knew war first-hand. He knew that Malta might at any time find herself under attack from sea and air. As a technical officer he realised better than most the totally inadequate resources that were then on the island to meet such attacks if they came. If they did come, they were in for a bad time on little Malta, and they would have to dig their toes in and fight with what they had, making a very little go a very long way. So Collins turned to and made sure that everything within his sphere of command was in first-class order, men and machines. After two years of hard driving he thought that at last he could boast that his mechanics and workshops were as efficient as anybody could make them.

He was one of that hard core of men upon whom Britain have leaned so heavily in past emergencies, hard-working, conscientious, patriotic men, who have done their duty, and more than their duty in relatively humble positions well out of the limelight so that the wheels of the nation's effort could be kept turning. And Collins did so with a smile, for his ample sense of humour made him realise that his efforts, although appreciated by those around him, would never be acclaimed in the pages of fame and glory. He was a man of ebullient energy, a man hard enough, and at the same time human enough, to get the best out of men and machines, a man who made things go. And to the AOC in Malta he soon made himself indispensable.

So much so that when, on mobilisation for war, most of the RAF technical personnel, together with the majority of the aircraft, were dispersed from the island, Collins was retained. If war should come he was one of those who could not be spared. He was one of a picked staff, most of them NCOs, who were kept at Kalafrana to supervise the Maltese civilian employees. The Aircraft Repair Section was thereafter kept fully employed maintaining patrolling flying boats, until these were all sent to Gibraltar at the end of 1939, and any aircraft using the island as a transit base. Four Swordfish aircraft found excessively unserviceable on mobilisation were brought 'serviceable'.

The Maltese civilian employees of the Aircraft Repair Section consisted, for the most part, of ex-dockyard apprentices and ex-Maltese Auxiliary Air Force men, most of the latter having seen service with the RAF in the Middle East between the years 1918 and 1925. These mechanics had worked on aircraft continuously over a period of twenty years, and from the spring of 1938 they had been organised in specialist 'gangs', in readiness for the war that seemed likely to overtake the island, under the officer and NCOs who were to supervise them. Collins and his Warrant Officer had both served with some of these men twenty years before. Altogether the Section entered the war already a very experienced and efficient team. It was just as well for Malta that they were, for they were to be sorely tested in the months, and most particularly in the immediate weeks, to come. The mechanics were a likeable crowd, loyal, efficient, hard-working and, as time proved only too well, willing to take risks and work until they dropped.

Collins had under him as NCO-in-charge Engines Sergeant F. H. Dimmer, a very experienced man who had formerly been attached to the Engine Repair Section. Like Collins, he had no illusions of what war would mean to a vulnerable, unprotected island like Malta. The two men had hit it off from the first and worked together well.

One day earlier in April the ARS phone rang. Collins lifted the receiver. 'Flying Officer Collins speaking.'

'Oh, Michie here.' It was the Commanding Office of Kalafrana, Wing Commander Michie. 'Look, Collins, there are four cased naval Gladiators in our store. Unpack, erect, and get them to Hal Far as fast as you can go. All right? We're going to have a Fighter Flight after all, if the AOC can find the pilots and get them trained in time. But it's up to us to give him the aircraft and in double quick time. So get going. All right?'

'Yes, sir.' Collins put the phone down. Crikey. Just like that. And what do we do for spares? Oh well, never argue in the RAF, just do what you're told. He lifted the phone again and got hold of Warrant Officer Paynor.

'Hello. Is that you, Paynor? The CO's just been on the blower. Get cracking at once and muster four unpacking and erecting teams. We've got to uncrate four of those Sea-Gladiators on the slipway, assemble them and send them up to Hal Far. We're going to have a Station Fighter Flight.... What? Yes, I know, but there it is. Start right away and don't stop till the last Gladiator is at Hal Far. OK? Right?'

So Sea-Gladiators N.5520, N.5519, N.5531 and N.5524 were uncrated, assembled, and trundled up the road to Hal Far – and into history.

As soon as the AOC's scheme for a Station Fighter Flight became known, volunteers came forward from the few pilots still left on the island.

One of these was Maynard's own Personal Assistant, Flight Lieutenant George Burges. Burges had recently made the first landing on the new airfield at Luqa. He was by training a flying-boat man but was convinced that he could turn himself into a fighter pilot without too much trouble. So he became a member of the new Station Fighter Flight, Hal Far. He retained his job as Personal Assistant to the AOC, however, and for some weeks led an extremely hectic life, shuttlecocking between Hal Far and Valetta.

In all, seven volunteers were eventually selected. None of them were fighter pilots. The entry in the Operations Record Book of Hal Far for 19 April 1940 reads:

Four Sea-Gladiators from Kalafrana issued to Station
Flight as equipment for Station Fighter Flight. As soon

as these machines were rigged and flight tested, R/T and armament training was commenced. The following were the officer personnel of Station Fighter Flight:

    Squadron Leader A. C. Martin
    Flight Lieutenant G. Burges (attached from HQ, Med)
    Flight Lieutenant P. G. Keeble
    Flying Officer W. J. Woods
    Flying Officer J. L. Waters
    Pilot Officer P. B. Alexander

Flight Lieutenant Peter Keeble, a short-service-commission officer, was taken from the original Station Flight at Hal Far, as also was Flying Officer W. J. (Timber) Woods, an Irishman. Another member of Station Flight not listed in the Operations Book was Flying Officer P. W. Hartley, who had been a Staff Pilot in No 3 Anti-Aircraft Co-operation Unit. From the same unit came Flying Officer John Waters. Pilot Officer 'Pete' Alexander, a Canadian, had been attached to an Experimental Flight of Queen Bee radio-controlled aircraft. Commanding the new Station Fighter Flight was Squadron Leader 'Jock' Martin, also from the staff at Hal Far.

They all found the Gladiators a bit strange to fly. To begin with, traces of their former owners were very apparent. They still retained their Y-shaped deck hooks underneath the fuselage between the fixed undercarriage and the tail, and the air-speed indicator was calibrated in knots.

George Burges thought that the funniest thing about the Gladiator was its propeller.

'You just sit there with that big, two-bladed wooden job ticking round in slow tempo. Nothing seems to be happening out there – just this enormous fan going clonkity-clonk in front of you.'

But they all agreed that the Gladiators were first-class aeroplanes, even if they were a bit long in the tooth. They were the last, and best, of the biplane fighters.

'The others all had their nasty little ways,' said John

Waters later, 'but the Gladiator had no vices at all.'

'Climb like bats out of hell,' said another pilot. 'A kid could fly 'em.'

An entry in the Operations Record Book covering the next ten days runs as follows:

'29.4.40 AM: Anxiety as to Italy's probable intentions and the opening up of the war in Norway caused some modification of the usual training commitments of the units of this station during this month, and necessitated a certain amount of operational training being given to pilots who were completely unversed in operational work.'

That meant Station Fighter Flight. It was heavily impressed upon the pilots of the Gladiators that their aircraft were more precious than rubies, and that anyone damaging them would be very unpopular. There was a standing rule to treat the old ladies with the greatest care. Flying time was jealously hoarded, and a 30-minute practice flight a thing to gloat over. They practised formation flying, height climbs and gunnery, but on the whole training was scanty, particularly in the air-to-air combat that they could expect as soon as the sirens went in Malta.

Meanwhile the Service heads on the island were busy working out plans to deal with the emergency, should it arise within the next few weeks. By the look of events in Europe and Scandinavia this seemed likely. Lack of fighter aircraft was not the only problem worrying the AOC and his staff. The difficulties of defending a small island like Malta from air attack were so great that many people in high positions thought the island indefensible.

To begin with, the three airfields and the dockyards around Grand Harbour, which formed the four main military targets, were all confined in the eastern half of this compact target island, and were linked by a puzzle of narrow, winding roads that were not much more than country lanes. Then the conditions of the airfields left much to be desired. Hal Far, down in the north-east corner of the island, was the oldest of the three and was just a narrow strip of grass bordered by rock and ravine. Takali, the next oldest field, lay on the cultivated plain that stretched between Rabat, the ancient Maltese capital, and Valetta. It was well known to Italian civil airline pilots, who had been using it for some time. Takali, dominated by hills on three sides, had been built on the site of an ancient lake and its grass surface became boggy very quickly in bad weather. Both Hal Far and Takali, grass airfields without runways, suffered from this disadvantage. Rain was their worst enemy.

If these two fields became waterlogged there was only one other to which aircraft could be diverted. This was Luqa, the newest and best of the three. Luqa had runways. This airfield had been built on high ground a mile or so inland, on a site dominating Grand Harbour and the dockyards, and its construction had been a triumph of persistence and ingenuity. Designed as a bomber airfield, it was incomplete when Air Commodore Maynard arrived on the island. From the first, the new AOC showed his confidence in the ability of Malta to mount a powerful striking force in the event of war by persevering with the building of Luqa. The difficulties were formidable in the extreme. The whole site for the airfield had to be levelled from hills, quarries and nullahs, and there were no proper tools for airfield construction on the island. Primitive Maltese labouring methods and British ingenuity triumphed in the end, however. In this way were laid the 1,200 yards of tarmac forming the longest runway on the island. The airfield was cramped in closely by villages, which pushed their farms right up to the edge of the airfield perimeter, grabbing every possible inch of Malta's scarce, priceless soil. Land for farming was so limited on the little island that station commanders were hard put to disperse their aircraft properly. But Air Commodore Maynard had plans to deal with that difficulty as well.

Malta was so small that any sort of defence in depth was out of the question. War would bring immediate heavy air attacks on the three airfields to put them out of action and prevent any chance of opposition in the air, and there were no reserve fields if these three were bombed out of use. In England, soon to face the Battle of Britain, there were airfields in the Midlands and in Yorkshire from which aircraft could be brought up to reinforce the southern airfields, and to which exhausted squadrons could be diverted. There were no Yorkshires in an island seventeen miles by nine – just three airfields, and all of there in the front line. Enemy aircraft could be over the island almost before the defenders knew they were there, even with the radar equipment installed on the island. How long would three little airfields last – and four old fighters, even supposing they were effective at all – against the might of the Regia Aeronautica? The answer seemed all too unpleasantly obvious.

If it were, the pilots of Station Fighter Flight seemed unaware of it as they practised their climbs and interceptions. In spite of the warning to handle the Gladiators with caution, it became the form to rag the Senior Air Staff Officer by indulging in aerobatics whenever things threatened to become tedious.

One day Martin came into the mess. The others, draped listlessly round the room, noticed a twinkle in his eye.

'Look chaps – when we scramble this afternoon, let's have a bit of fun. Life's getting a bit dull. Tell you what – as soon as you've grabbed enough height I'll call you up and suggest all sorts of outrageous and hair-raising aerobatics. You play up to me and we'll put on a tremendous act, pretend we're going through the whole ruddy repertoire – stall turns, loops in formation, the whole damn shoot.'

The lethargy vanished. Anything to relieve the monotony.

'Sound idea,' said Burges. 'Somebody can scream out "Look out, I'm going to hit you."'

'Yes,' said someone else. 'Give the old boy the idea we're out of control or something. He's bound to be listening into the R/T.'

'That's the idea,' Jock said enthusiastically. When we come in you two do stall turns and I'll do a loop and try to land off it. You never know, we might even get away with it.'

'Poor old SASO,' said Peter Keeble. 'He'll be having kittens down here.'

A few minutes later they were airborne and circling round the southern coast of the island. Jock called them up.

'Hello, Red Section. We'll try a loop in formation.' A few seconds went by. 'Right, diving now. Speed about two-eighty. All right. *Over we go!* ... Get in closer, Red Two, close it up for God's sake... OK, OK, hold it at that ... *hold it!* ... phew, I thought we'd *both* bought it then.' The 'manoeuvre' finished, he called up again.

'OK, chaps, that wasn't too bad. Now let's try a roll... Look out! *Look out!* You're going to collide, *you're going to collide!* Oh my God, I can't look, I can't look...'

When they landed the wretched Senior Air Staff Officer, who had pictured the air defence of Malta lying in a heap of smoking wreckage, tore them all off a strip so enormous that they never ventured to repeat the experiment.

So the training of Malta's fighter defence went on. Then, only ten days after the Gladiators had been delivered to Hal Far, the Operations Record Book reads:

'29.4.40 AM: Station Fighter Flight temporarily disbanded and Sea-Gladiators dismantled and returned to Kalafrana.'

That morning Flying Officer Collins at Kalafrana had lifted the phone again. Once more it was the Station CO.

'Michie here. Oh, Collins, it seems the Admiralty have allotted the Gladiators to Alexandria and a ship is calling to collect them, so get them back from Hal Far, will you, and into their cases again as quickly as you can. Ring me when you've finished the packing.'

'Very good, sir.' He sent for Warrant Officer Paynor.

'Paynor, away towing party and get the Gladiators back from Hal Far. Repack them – carefully. Some poor devils may have to erect them in a hurry, under war conditions.'

So it was only a dream after all. Malta had lost her fighter defence. This blow, coupled with the news of the fall of Norway, cast a cloud of gloom and despondency over Hal Far. The Gladiators departed from the airfield at a time when a handful of other Gladiators were fighting their last desperate fight from a frozen Norwegian lake. Some of these succeeded in landing aboard the *Glorious*, only to be lost with the carrier when she was sunk shortly afterwards.

It was lunchtime on the 30th, the day after the order had been given to repack the Gladiators at Kalafrana. The weary packing party were just securing the doors of the fourth Gladiator case when a man rushed up.

'The CO wants Flying Officer Collins on the phone.' Collins hurried to his office and picked up the phone.

'Flying Officer Collins speaking.'

'Michie here. How goes the packing?'

'Just finished, sir. The last bolts just being put on the last case now, sir. I was just about to phone when you called me.'

'That was quick. Damn good show. The thing is, er … I suppose you're all ready for lunch?'

'Just about, sir.'

'Yes, well, go and have lunch, have a nice lunch – then unpack the lot again and get 'em back to Hal Far as quick as you can. The AOC has got permission to keep them after all and they look like being needed any time now. I'll come along and say a few words to the men.'

The CO came, explained the position to the tired men and, after a quick meal, the cases were opened up once more.

Rigging an aircraft is not a simple job. It is rather like piecing together an enormous jigsaw puzzle of wires, struts, cables, wheels, wings and controls, with the difference that the jigsaw puzzle in this case will have to be put into the air and flown. It took mankind several centuries before he could give even a clumsy imitation of a bird. Even now he isn't half as good at it as the most carelessly rigged swallow, and if his artificial wings are not put together properly he will at best fly very clumsily, and at worst break his neck. As the RAF manual said (AP3042A, Section 2, Principles of Air Frame Construction and Rigging):

'19. General.

It is of extreme importance that an aeroplane shall be correctly rigged. Depending on the type, it will be found that parts can be fitted (apparently correctly) at slightly wrong angles, or slightly twisted and bent. These errors may not be obvious without inspection, but will cause the aeroplane to fly badly. Unlike other machines, the aeroplane structure is fairly flexible, and incorrect adjustment of bracing wires, for example, will make it lopsided and unsymmetrical without the usual indication of incorrect assembly – the need for excessive force.'

Collins's men, well-trained by him in the first place, by now had some experience of rigging a Gladiator. There wasn't much need to worry that *their* product would be 'lopsided and unsymmetrical' or that there would be 'the need for excessive force' – except on the part of their Commanding Officer if they did make a mistake.

But there was a need, a very urgent need, for excessive speed. Where speed is involved at the height of a crisis, error tends to creep in. But nobody must make any error – not with these priceless machines.

The aircraft were all packed, ready for despatch, one aircraft to a crate. Inside each crate the fuselage, stripped of wings, tailplane, propeller and wheels, rested on its undercarriage legs, packed round with all the rest of its parts, the fuselage having been coated with a preservative preparation and the engine with an anti-rust grease. After lunch the bolts were taken off, the first case opened, and the Gladiator's fuselage manhandled out once more. Then the onerous job of rigging proceeded by steps.

First the wheels were fixed on. Then a detailed inspection of the fuselage was made to see that everything was correct and in place. Next the tail unit had to be attached to the fuselage, tailplane and fin, rudder and elevators, and the whole unit checked for possible distortion. After this came the biggest job of all – fitting the main planes and adjusting them. One set of planes had to be erected at a time, first the port side, say, then the starboard. All control cables were first checked for freedom and attachment bolts for fitting. Then each plane in turn, lower plane first, had to be lifted into position and bolted to the fuselage. The landing or 'anti-lift' wires, those running diagonally upwards towards the fuselage, helping to support the wing when the aircraft was on the ground, were put on. Now the upper plane corresponding to the lower one already in position had to be fitted. For this a trestle had to be put under the lower plane beneath the position of the interplane struts to take the weight and keep it firm. The top plane, supported on a cradle clear of the ground, was then made ready and the struts fitted into position on its undersurface. It was then slung into its correct position, bolted to the centre-section, which was fixed to the fuselage already, and the struts fitted to the bottom plane. Then the 'flying' or 'lift' wires, which run diagonally downwards towards the fuselage and helped in flight to transfer the lift from the wing to the fuselage, were fixed in position, followed by the incidence wires – the cross bracing wires between the struts that served to maintain the planes at the correct stagger and angle of incidence and prevent twisting. One set of planes was then in position, and it simply sufficed for the sweating mechanics to do the whole thing all over again for the planes on the other side.

With wings attached, they had to be tested for dihedral, angle of incidence and stagger, and the wires adjusted for correct tension. Finally, the flying control system checked and the propeller fitted, the aircraft was given a final overall check before Collins would pronounce it properly rigged.

It was a tedious, tiring, delicate job. And that was only number one. There were three more yet. But Collins and his men worked like galley slaves and inside an hour Gladiator

N.5520 was being trundled up the narrow, dusty road towards Hal Far, ready to be flight-tested again. The great care with which the aircraft had been dismantled previously had helped a great deal when it came to reassembling them.

'Oh well, I can take a joke,' said Collins. 'We were the "poor devils" who "might have to erect them in a hurry" after all. What a life!'

And by the time the fourth Gladiator had been erected again, the Aircraft Repair Section felt they could do the job blindfolded.

'It's just like Meccano,' said Collins.

On 5 May the Operations Book thankfully records, 'Sea-Gladiators returned to Hal Far from Kalafrana.'

Fighter training went on. Fighter Flight had become a happy little outfit. The pilots had got to know each other reasonably well by now and individual characteristics had become noticeable.

There was Timber Woods's Irish superstition, for example. Timber thought the colour green terribly unlucky. It so happened that one of the Gladiators had part of its fuselage painted green, and Timber would do anything to avoid flying this particular machine. But Timber was rather a lone wolf and difficult to get to know. He had come up the hard way and had a much rougher background than the others. As a result he was not by any means as sure of himself as his rather restrained behaviour seemed to indicate. Timber would always talk soccer while the others followed rugger. He was not a natural pilot, but full of courage.

Peter Keeble was an example of the best type of Royal Air Force short-service officer. He was energetic and absolutely fearless, if a trifle hot-headed. He had a brother in the RAF in England of whom he was very fond. Peter owned a little Fiat 'Toppelino' that he had bought in Malta, and it was a familiar sight to see him driving it flat out between Hal Far and his flat at Bursibbuggia on the coast. He would often go sailing, too, with his attractive wife,

Lorna. One of his and the other pilots' favourite haunts was Peter Dowdall's hotel at Bursibbuggia. The pilots of Station Fighter Flight were often to be seen there, lounging in the sun on the balcony at the back, overlooking the peaceful water of the bay. There the proprietor, a beaming, genial man, half Irish, half Maltese, would dispense his notable, open-handed hospitality. 'You're all my guests today,' he would say, his big, chubby face alight with the enormous joy of food and drink, laughter and friendship under the sun.

John Waters was a tall, quiet, good-looking young man who affected a rather languid, casual air. He was lucky in that he alone of the new flight had actually flown Gladiators before. His parent unit on Malta was No 3 Anti-Aircraft Co-operation Unit, but shortly before, while the *Glorious* had been in harbour and her squadrons ashore at Hal Far, he had flown, quite unofficially, with No 802 Fighter Squadron from the carrier. By now the Fleet Air Arm had been handed back to the Navy and 802's Sea-Gladiators were flown by naval officers.

One day, 802's Commanding Officer, Lieutenant Commander 'Monkey' Bryant, said to Waters, 'John, how would you like a trip in a Gladiator?' Waters had been longing for a chance to try his hand in a Gladiator, so he said, in his quiet, rather diffident manner, that he 'wouldn't mind', and Bryant promised him a chance as soon as possible.

Shortly afterwards 802 were doing a mock stand-by. On a ring of a telephone they were to get airborne immediately. John Waters was allocated one of the aircraft. Then they got the 'scramble'. The Gladiators were dispersed all round the airfield, and Waters had already realised, from the position of his aircraft, that if he wanted to scramble quickly he would have to take off downwind – in a strange aircraft, a fighter, that was a good deal faster and trickier than the machines he had been used to. But he knew he had to try and put one over on the Navy. He saw the naval pilots running to their aircraft. 'Laughing up their bloody sleeves,' he thought. But Waters was a natural pilot. Without any trouble at all he roared off downwind and was easily the first in the air. After that Bryant said, 'Well, you'll have to stay with us, chum.'

And so he did, practising all sorts of hair-raising aerobatics all over the Maltese sky. A favourite evolution of 802 was to dive in a close 'follow-my-leader' formation, with each machine fighting to hold its position against the slipstream of the one in front. They practised night formation, too, a risky business, each aircraft having only one small blue light fixed to a strut.

Waters flew with 802 until *Glorious* left Malta, then went back to flying Swordfish with No 3 AACU. He didn't expect to get a chance of flying a Gladiator again.

Peter Hartley was the 'farmer' of Hal Far. For some time before he joined Station Fighter Flight he had been attracted to the idea of taking up agriculture. To him there seemed to be a connection between flying and farming. He knew that if he left the Air Force the other was the only sort of life he wanted: the idea of working in an office all day was utterly abhorrent to one who spent his time in the freedom of the air and sunlight. Flying was reality to him, and deep down in his mind he felt that to farm the land, to be out in all weathers, to grow food, to raise crops and cattle, would be real, too, natural and satisfying. He was always planning vaguely how to raise enough money to buy a small farm in the south of England. Then it came to him that he might start a little 'farm' here and now, on Hal Far. The Station Commander, 'Ginger' O'Sullivan, was all in favour of the idea, so Hartley went to the Malta Government Experimental Farm, selected one or two pigs, ducks and chickens and took them back to the airfield. Here he first got himself two assistants, Airman Wood, who had been a farmer's boy in Yorkshire and knew all about pigs, and a tough Maltese labourer who was keen on farmwork. They built a few pens and got the 'farm' going. Between flights it became Hartley's main occupation.

He and John Waters became close friends. They made a trio with the RAF doctor, Freddie Moore, a wild, belligerent little man, in civilian life a brilliant plastic surgeon. He was a man who hated discipline. He knew his job and that was enough for him. Moore was mad to fly and persuaded Waters and Hartley to teach him. They used to take him up in the Station Magister, taking it in turns, and Freddie soon picked it up, although he persisted in going into a climbing left-hand turn as soon as he took off. He, Hartley and Waters were the 'Three Musketeers' of Hal Far.

The baby of the flight, Pete Alexander, was the forerunner of a long line of Canadians who were destined to fly fighters from Malta in the years ahead. Pete was excitable, highly strung and given to a rather rash 'couldn't care less' attitude in the air.

Jock Martin, the CO, seemed on the surface to be what later came to be taken by the general public as a 'typical' RAF officer – the good party type, handlebar moustache, whisky-tenor voice and a spicy vocabulary, much given to 'wizard prangs', 'shocking types' and 'absolute clots'. But underneath the greasepaint of buffoonery Jock was a sensitive man, and a man of great courage. He had had a bad crash in a Fairey Gordon some years before and walked with a limp as a result. Jock was getting on in years for fighter work, but he insisted on flying as much as anyone else.

He was a man who managed to wring a laugh out of any situation in which he was involved, however unpleasant. Landing one day in his Gladiator, somewhat out of wind, he had a slight argument with a large packing case that abutted on to the flight path. The crash turned the aircraft over on to its side and it was quickly surrounded by eager rescuers armed with fire extinguishers and axes. But there was no sign of Jock. Suddenly he appeared in the rear ranks of the would-be rescuers, looking immaculate in his white overalls and smoking his pipe.

'Hello,' he said, raising his eyebrows, 'what's the flap?'

As May wore on a greater sense of tension and urgency entered the atmosphere at Hal Far. Armour-plating was fitted to the Gladiators and training was intensified. The Records

Book begins to talk of 'practice blackouts' and 'ack-ack units reorganised', and on the 8th of the month:

> 'Raid and Interception exercises carried out in cooperation with HQ Mediterranean War Room.'

Two days later the news came through that Germany had invaded Holland, Belgium and Luxembourg. The immediate result at Hal Far was quite striking, as the faithful barometer of the Operations Record Book clearly reflects:

> '11.5.40 AM: Owing to use of parachute troops and top carriers by Germany in Holland it was considered necessary to block the aerodrome with motor vehicles. One flight path was kept open for aircraft to operate from: this could be closed by vehicles when aircraft were not flying.'

The wide expanse of grass was covered with buses, carozzins, old cars, cranes, packing cases and any old junk that would fill in space. The take-off and landing strip lay among these obstacles, blocked by mobile vehicles that could be backed out of the way when flying took place. The Gladiators had only this narrow strip to use, even if there was a 90-degree crosswind. Naturally the rate of minor accidents to aircraft increased. In one practice scramble over the hurdles Peter Hartley came to grief.

They took off that day into a strong crosswind and in doing so Hartley struck a packing-case with his starboard wheel. When he was airborne he called up Alexander, who was flying alongside him, and asked him to edge in closer and report on the damage. Alexander was rather excited, and Hartley was, as he put it later, 'not without apprehension'. The Canadian duly made his inspection, then was heard over the R/T to say:

'Gee boy, you're gonna be goddam lucky to get out of this!'

Hartley approached the field again in some trepidation. He found the flight path all right but the instant that his wheels touched down his machine overturned, scraping the nose of the aircraft and smashing the propeller.

Apart from incidents of this kind and the routine of training, time passed fretfully for the men of Fighter Flight. When they were not in the air practising gunnery and interceptions and the like, that is to say when they could not persuade, cajole or bribe Control into letting them fly, they would pass the time by helping to belt up ammunition for the guns.

No one knew when the fun was going to start in earnest, but they all guessed it would be soon. An infallible barometer was the Alittoria flying boat, which still came in every day. The pilots argued that if one day it failed to arrive, that would be a fairly good indication that the big show was on. Bets were laid as to the probable non-appearance of the flying boat on any particular day, and a great deal of money changed hands, not to mention free pints of beer consumed by lucky punters. Everyone knew about this and no one was very surprised therefore when the following fragment of chit-chat was overheard from the three aircraft airborne on that day.

The conversation was introduced by the inevitable version of 'Here we go round the mulberry bush', whistled by George Burges over the R/T.

Burges: 'Hello, Red One. All right, Jock. I'll be round for my five bob.'

Martin: 'What, old boy? I can't hear you. My R/T's gone u.s. again.'

Burges: '*My five bob*. Remember? We had a bet. And there's the Alittoria kite now, still going about her peaceful business among us.'

Martin: 'To hell With Mussolini, he's costing me money.'

Alexander: 'Hello, Red One. Say, skipper, what say we beat him up a little? Let's go down and dog-fight him.'

Martin: 'Christ on a bicycle! Hold your horses! What happens if a brass hat sees your Canadian capers? Just a little patience, old boy. You'll soon be getting all the dog-fighting you want – with Macchi 200s!'

The war situation was deteriorating rapidly. The battle for France was as good as lost and the British and French were being driven back towards the coast. At Hal Far, on 15 May:

'Pistols and two magazines of ammunition issued to officers and senior NCOs... 'A' Coy, 2nd Batt Royal West Kent Regiment attached to Hal Far for aerodrome defence and commenced to wire the aerodrome boundary.'

By this time it had been decided that, because there were no spares for the four Gladiators, the obvious policy would be to fly three of them and keep one in immediate reserve, then stand by with all available materials and equipment and rely upon the skill of the craftsmen. It was thought that, if all three operational aircraft were damaged on a raid, the two most lightly damaged machines could be repaired by as many skilled men as could efficiently be put on the job, and the most heavily damaged aircraft replaced by the immediate reserve machine. Then work would proceed day and night until the badly damaged aircraft was serviceable again.

From 20 May three Gladiators maintained a continuous stand-by at 2 minutes' notice during the daylight hours, from 5 o'clock in the morning until 8 at night, while one Swordfish aircraft of No 3 Anti-Aircraft Cooperation Unit's Operational Flight stood by at 15 minutes' notice day and night. All gun posts on the aerodrome were manned and the aerodrome defences brought to a full state of readiness. Training for the fighters continued and every minute so spent became priceless.

'21.5.40 AM: During morning stand-to, Gladiators carried out a practice shoot-up of aerodrome.'

This was to test the aerodrome defences against a semblance of the reality they could expect any day. Six days later...

'27.5.40 AM: Curfew imposed from 2300-0500 night. All personnel not on specific duty and in possession of pass forbidden the roads on pain of being shot at during those hours.'

Outside the airfields the whole of Malta prepared for the coming storm. Arrangements were made for the dispersal of the population of Valetta in the event of heavy air raids. Ancient catacombs deep down in the rock were taken over as shelters and additional shelters were cut out of the soft, limestone rock of the island, rock which is soft internally and easy to cut, but which hardens quickly on exposure to the air. Conscription had already been introduced, and the training of Maltese recruits for artillery and infantry units was now accelerated. A careful check was made on food and fuel supplies.

When would it come? When would Mussolini strike? In the empty air above a restless city, the pilots of Fighter Flight stared from their cramped cockpits at the thin, faint beaches of Sicily, just sixty miles away.

On the night of 10 June Air Chief Marshal Brooke-Popham was dining with the Governor, General Dobbie, and the AOC at San Anton Palace. They were talking together when they heard the outer door, beyond the dining room, open, followed by a distant, muffled conversation. Then there was a knock at the door of their room.

'Come in,' said the Governor. The door opened and George Burges entered the room.

'Hello, Burges, what brings you here?' asked Maynard.

General Dobbie said quietly, 'I think I know.'

'Yes, sir,' said Burges. 'Mussolini has declared war.'

'Has he, by Jove!' exclaimed Brooke-Popham. 'Have you had any dinner, my boy?'

'No, sir,' said the excited Burges.

'Well, you'd better sit down and have some. You can't fight a war on an empty stomach, you know.'

So he sat down at the councils of the mighty and ate a hearty dinner. Then he went back to Hal Far to get some sleep and wait for whatever was to come.

CHAPTER FOUR

Faith, Hope and Charity

At Hal Far on the morning of the 11th, the pilots waited and three fighters stood fuelled up and ready out on the flight path.

They had been at readiness since four o'clock, hanging around by the aircraft expecting the klaxon to scream at any moment.

'This is a fine old lark, isn't it?' said Martin.

'Um.' Burges was deep in thought. A few minutes later –

'I'm sure somebody told me there was a war on.'

A minute passed.

'Personally, I think the whole thing's a ruddy leg-pull.'

'I wish something would bloody well hap–'

The klaxon screeched. Sirens howled in the distance. A door slammed open and a voice yelled:

'Scramble the fighters!'

They were already running to the aircraft, with Burges leading by a short head.

He reached his machine, climbed in, pulled the side flap of the cockpit up and adjusted his harness. Reaching down he gave the engine seven or eight dopes on the priming pump. The ground crew pressed the starting button. Burges pressed the self-starter. The engine exploded into life at once. He opened up the throttle and roared down the field.

In a matter of minutes all three were airborne and climbing flat out. Martin opened the proceedings.

'Banjo from Red One, Red Section airborne.'

Down below, Control answered him.

'Red One from Banjo. Bandits approaching Grand Harbour from north.'

'Banjo from Red One. Your message received and understood.'

A minute went by.

'Red One from Banjo. Guns engaging bandits.'

Burges said tensely, 'I can see them. Look, smoke over Hal Far.'

'I can see bomb splashes out there beyond the breakwaters,' said Martin's voice, waving and crackling over the R/T. 'Rotten shooting, they'll have to do better than that. OK chaps, let's get amongst 'em! *Tally-ho!*'

They opened their throttles and drove the Gladiators through the sky above Valetta as far as their old legs would carry them. The old aircraft quivered and shook as they charged, the early sun glinting on their cockpit hoods.

Burges had the best aircraft and began to outstrip the others. He saw a bunch of Italian SM 79 bombers going away to the south-west of the island and circling round to head for home. Climbing hard he managed to cut off a corner and eventually intercepted the last formation when they were about halfway back to Sicily.

Coming in on their starboard quarter he held his fire to be sure of a hit, then gave the nearest bomber a few quick, sharp bursts. He saw his bullets go home.

However, as soon as he banked away to come in for another attack he realised that the Italians were drawing away from him. As he put it later:

'As soon as I opened up, the Italians poured on the coal
and the Gladiator just couldn't catch up with them.'

It was a bit of an anti-climax, but it was only the opening gambit. No one expected the Gladiators to shoot anything down – especially on their first pass at the enemy. Indeed, most people looked on the whole Gladiator effort as a mere token gesture, a thumbing of the nose at Mussolini and a fillip for Maltese morale. The pilots knew that SM 79s were faster than their own aircraft and they knew that they would have to produce extra-special form to overcome the handicap.

But one important thing they had accomplished. The

Italians and, for that matter, the Maltese too, now knew that Malta had fighters to defend her. They had seen them, they had felt them, and they knew that they would be waiting when they came back.

As soon as he landed, Burges was sent for by the Governor and the AOC. They both regretted that he had been unable to shoot anything down and put their heads together to try and think of a way of improving matters.

'Well, I'm glad you got a shot at them anyway,' Maynard said. At least it will show them we've got some fighters and mean to use them.'

The Governor agreed. Yes, I think you are to be congratulated on getting your attack in when you did,' he said. 'What's your own verdict on it?'

Burges answered at once. 'Well, sir, as they're faster than we are, I think our only chance is to scramble and climb as fast as we can and hope that we are four or five thousand feet above them when they arrive over the island. It's no good trying to overhaul them. We shall just have to get into the air quicker and climb faster – somehow.'

'Yes,' said Maynard. We shall have to get more speed out of them by some means or other. I'll talk it over with my Command Engineer Officer right away.'

The siren had gone at 6.49 that morning. In that first raid the Italians had come over in two 'V' formations of seven and three, the first wave meant for the docks around Grand Harbour, the second for Hal Far. This raid was merely a softener, a foretaste to the Maltese and the men of the airfields and dockyards of what they could expect later in greater measure. What was it Douhet had said?

'...a people who are bombed today as they were bombed yesterday, *who know they will be bombed again tomorrow* and see no end to their martyrdom...'

But tomorrow the Gladiators would be there too, and they meant to do better next time.

The Italians did not wait until tomorrow. They came over eight times in all during the first day. The second time they came they paid a tribute to the Gladiators by bringing fighter escorts, CR 42s and Macchi 200s.

The last raiders of the day came over at 7.25 in the evening. Fighter Flight took off. What happened when the old Gladiators met modern Macchis, Timber Woods told in his combat report on the fight.

'We sighted a formation of five S 79 enemy aircraft approaching Valetta at a height of approximately 15,000 feet. We climbed until we were slightly above them, and then Red Two delivered an attack from astern. The enemy had turned out to sea. I delivered an attack from astern, and got in a good burst at a range of approximately 200 yards. My fire was returned. I then broke away and returned over the island at approximately 11,000 feet, south of Grand Harbour.

While still climbing to gain height, I observed another formation of five enemy aircraft approaching. They were at about the same height as myself. I attacked from abeam at about 150 yards and got in one good burst. The enemy started firing at me long before I opened up. This formation broke slightly but left me well behind when I tried to get in an attack from astern.

Just after that, when again climbing to gain more height, I suddenly heard machine-gun fire from behind me. I immediately went into a steep left-hand turn and saw a single-engine fighter diving and firing at me. For quite three minutes I circled as tightly as possible and got the enemy in my sight. I got in a good burst, full deflection shot, and he went down in a steep dive with black smoke pouring from his tail. I could not follow him down, but he appeared to go into the sea.'

This report tells its own story of coolness, resolution and superior skill. Woods had proved that a Gladiator could outfly and outfight a more modern opponent, once it could hold the enemy to a definite engagement. He had destroyed a fighter. The bombers, however, had been able to do their work and get away without loss... '*This formation broke slightly but left me well behind*' ... They would have to do something about that.

However, the importance of this victory was not to be underestimated. The effect of the destruction of an enemy aircraft in full view of the people of an island that everyone, friend and foe alike, except a small handful of men, had thought to be defenceless, was enormous. The confidence of those engaged in the defence of Malta soared, and the morale of the civilian population rocketed to a height from which it never again descended.

Maynard's faith in the ability of the RAF to defend Malta successfully had been justified. He and all the men concerned with the creation and operation of Station Fighter Flight had proved the sceptics wrong. The Gladiators had not been shot out of the air. In fact, they had had the impudence to attack and intimidate the invincible armada that was to have smashed Malta. They and the anti-aircraft gunners between them had taught Mussolini a lesson.

No, Mussolini was not in Valetta yet. It now remained to be seen whether the defenders could keep it up. The sceptics on both sides talked of a flash in the pan. The RAF was quietly confident that it could repeat the performance, although the hope in every mind was for more aircraft of a more modern type.

As night drew on Malta was able to take stock of the situation and count her casualties. One Fascist boast at least, that Malta would be taken in a day, had been thoroughly punctured. Malta was calm and ready.

The Royal Malta Artillery and the King's Own Malta Regiment stood firm at their posts in the coastal and aerodrome defences, and the men of the dockyard had carried on at their vital jobs all day.

In fact, volunteers from the dockyard had actually helped

to man the island's defences. The Naval Flag Officer in Charge in Malta, Vice-Admiral Sir Wilbraham Ford, had asked for men to come forward and swell the ranks of the army gunners, at that stage all too thin. The dockyard men had manned and fought the guns in their overalls.

The civilian population behaved with great coolness, save in their fury at Italian duplicity. There was no more talk of 'blood brothers' now, they noticed. Any Italian airman who had the misfortune to bail out over Malta might well expect to have his throat cut the instant his feet touched the ground.

In all, twenty-three civilians had been killed in the eight raids of that first day. If it had not been for the fighters there might have been many more. In addition to these dead, five soldiers of the Royal Malta Artillery had been killed when their gun had been put out of action by a direct shot on the fort at Saint Elmo, the place in which La Valette and his knights had made their triumphant stand in 1565.

Evacuation of the civilian population of Senglea, Vittoriosa and Cospicua, which, grouped as they were so closely round the naval dockyards, looked like becoming death traps in subsequent air-raids, began when the Italian raids commenced on the island, and eighty thousand people were successfully moved in one day to billets inland. They were bewildered at first, some of them people who had perhaps never gone before beyond the boundaries of the Three Cities, to whom a trip to Valetta itself was an exciting odyssey. One of these evacuees described the experience in a letter to a friend. He said:

'At eight o'clock this morning, a car arrived to take us to Rabat. We took with us sheets, blankets and other useful kitchen utensils. We even took with us a tin of kerosene. We tied two mattresses to the roof of the car and left without knowing where we are going. When we got to Ta Qali aerodrome we had to stop due to engine trouble. But soon after we were on our way again. We eventually found a house in a narrow street. It belonged to an old man and his two daughters. They were very pleased to put us up. One of the daughters was terrified every time she heard an air-raid signal. The other was just like my wife, never taking any notice of bombs. The old man used to burst out laughing whenever he saw anyone terrified. During an air-raid he used to go up on the roof to watch Italian planes coming in. I have always liked my own house but now all of a sudden I find myself imposing on other people, people whom I have never seen before.'

The bombs that had fallen on Hal Far had caused no damage to aircraft and very little to the airfield itself. The engineer officer there, Flying Officer 'Nobby' Clarke, who had seen much service aboard 'floating flatirons', as he called the aircraft carriers, rang up Flying Officer Collins at Kalafrana and told him he needed no assistance – so far.

Kalafrana too had come under attack. Several sticks of bombs straddled the Aircraft Repair Section, with all the anti-aircraft guns blazing away and men of the Royal Malta Regiment standing out in the open firing their rifles from the shoulder at the bombers. Unfortunately this was a waste of ammunition as the aircraft were, of course, far too high to be hit by a stray rifle bullet. Luckily no damage was done to the station except a few craters.

The gun posts at Kalafrana were commanded by technical NCOs and manned, for the most part, by Royal Air Force non-technical personnel. With the possibility of an attempted invasion in mind, Flying Officer Collins offered his services to the Station Commander as Station Defence Officer, selecting as his second-in-command Warrant Officer Purvis MM, who, by a very long arm of coincidence, had served in the same machine-gun battalion in France and Russia some twenty years earlier. His offer was thankfully accepted, the defence forces were adjusted, and positions consolidated. Collins was another man on Malta running two jobs at once.

Three bombers had been shot down during the day. It was to the chagrin of Station Fighter Flight that only one of these had fallen to them. They'd have to do better than that.

No one blamed the Gladiators themselves. Only a bad workman blames his tools, after all. But they did blame themselves. Obviously, they had a lot to learn. And they meant to learn it. Of course, the presence of those Macchis and CR 42s accompanying the later raids of the day was definitely one up to them. And one victory wasn't bad, for the first day. But it wasn't enough. Everyone put their heads together to see what changes could be made for the better.

First, the men of the Aircraft Repair Section got to work. Up to then the Gladiators had had the old constant-pitch wooden airscrews, Burges's 'big two-bladed wooden job ticking round in slow tempo'. These were removed and new propellers, of the three-bladed, two-speed variety, fitted. This meant that the pilots could switch to fine pitch for take off and to coarse pitch in the air, for flying and fighting with. With their new 'fans' they could count on a smoother, faster take-off than before, while their nautical air-speed indicators would show a few more knots. They might even be able to catch up with the SM 79s, or so they all hoped, touching wood.

This piece of improvisation was the same sort of last-minute rush job that maintenance crews had to do on Hurricanes in Britain, so that they could face the swarms of Messerschmitt 109s and 110s that came over.

Oh for just half a dozen of those Hurricanes at Hal Far! If a Gladiator could scare the Italians and make them drop their bombs in the sea, what might a Hurricane do?

But Hal Far had to make do with Gladiators and was thankful to have them. Kalafrana improvised, patched and generally 'duffed up' the old machines so that the pilots could have something fairly presentable to fight with. They knew that the men of Fighter Flight would have to take on fast, modern machines like the Macchi 200, which was an Italian equivalent of the Me 109. The situation was desperate so they worked like slaves and threw all the rules of aircraft care and maintenance away. 'Anything goes' was the watchword, anything to give the Gladiators more speed and keep them in the air. The AOC told his Command Engineer, Squadron Leader Louks, that he must think of something to improve the speed of the aircraft. Louks had an idea that might help, but it involved a gamble with time.

On the instrument panel of the Gladiator was a small red knob. In a tight corner, where a few extra miles per hour might save the day and the pilot's life, the pilot, with his throttle already wide open, could pull this knob. Doing this produced about an extra 10 pounds of boost in the engine. The aircraft then accelerated and gave him his extra speed. The effect of this was only meant to last for about 30 seconds, and the extra boost was only for use in extreme emergencies. Otherwise it was a privilege that could easily be abused. Too much flying at full throttle using the extra boost would be certain to overtax the engine and cause it to crack up.

But this *was* an emergency, and a more serious one than the designers of the Gladiator had ever envisaged. The old aircraft could not even catch the Italian bombers, let alone the fighters. They must be made to go faster.

There was only one thing to do. They would have to use the emergency boost, and the engines and controls would have to be modified so that the extra speed could be available at any time in the air without having to bother about pulling the red knob.

Sergeant Dimmer, as a good engineer, was very reluctant when the order reached him. He knew what running at maximum boost all the time would do to the engines in the long run. With all that extra strain on them it would be a short life and a gay one, without any spares to release worn-out parts. The Mercury was a first-class engine, but it had not been designed to work miracles. However, the AOC had as good as ordered a miracle, so Dimmer and his faithful Maltese mechanics had to turn themselves into magicians and give him one. 'Oh well,' thought Dimmer, 'we'll cross the next bridge when we come to it – when the engines actually start cracking up.' Until then it was his job to help give the pilots every fluke of speed he could squeeze out of the engines. They had to be able to catch the Italians and to break off and get away when the Macchis fell on them and the ammunition was gone. And there were only four of them. How long would they be able to keep them in the air? No spares, nothing, just four old aeroplanes pinched from the Navy! What an Air Force! But they would do what they could, and if anything could be done at all, then Kalafrana could be counted upon to do it.

So they went to work on the machines and modified them so that at full throttle the engines would produce every ounce of speed that was in them.

On the whole things were going well for Station Fighter Flight. They were not getting any more confirmed victories yet, but, thanks to the extra boost and their rapidly increasing experience, they were getting near enough to the bombers to damage some of them badly and break up their formation. More and more Italian bombardiers were dropping their bombs in the sea under pressure from the old biplanes. Some damaged bombers must have crashed and sunk before they could reach Sicilian shores, but only the sea could claim these as 'confirmed'...

One or two of the pilots had mascots in the shape of 'Christophers', given to them by Maltese to protect them against the Italians. They used to wear these in the air, and the Maltese would pray for their safety at the little shrines they had set up down in the rock shelters. There was a strong bond now between the Maltese and the pilots who flew above them, taking on fantastic odds in the defence of the island and its brave people. The people never forgot that these men had come forward to fight on their behalf in the air when no one in Malta had thought they had any defence in the air at all. If any of them were recognised in the streets of Valetta they were cheered and huge crowds followed them. When the sirens sounded and they took to the air, people forgot the danger of bombs to come out and watch them and marvel that they could go so bravely into such a fearful struggle.

By now everyone realised that they had in their midst a unique little unit that was making history every time its aircraft were airborne.

'You know, we ought to give them a name,' said Jock Martin, gazing reflectively at the three Gladiators lying out on the grass, with the petrol bowser filling up their tanks.

'What about "Faith, Hope and Charity"?' said John Waters.

'That's it,' said Jock. 'Faith, Hope and Charity.'

The name caught on. It spread beyond Hal Far to Valetta and soon over the whole island. It was soon on everybody's lips and all sorts of people claimed to have thought of it first. Every time the three Gladiators appeared in the sky, someone would point upwards and shout:

'There they go – Faith, Hope and Charity!'

The names fitted well into the solidly religious background of Maltese life. Nothing much more than a wry smile to most Englishmen at the time, at least, on the surface, they were symbolic of something deeper in the minds of many Maltese. To them it meant a great deal that the men and machines that defended them had been christened with the words of St Paul.

Of course everyone tried to out-do John Waters's inspired choice. But 'Pip, Squeak and Wilfred', and 'Freeman, Hardy and Willis' were nowhere in it. One hard-worked mechanic at Kalafrana came nearest. He called them 'Blood, Tears and Sweat'.

Gradually they were getting to know the loveable little ways of the enemy and the Italians in turn were getting wise to Faith, Hope and Charity's brighter tricks. On 17 June they started making use of one particular tactic to try and trap the Gladiators into their crossfire. On one raid that day one of the Gladiators attacked a formation of five SM 79s above Grand Harbour. As he came in astern one of the bombers detached itself from the rest of the formation and started to straggle some way behind the others. This was an open invitation to come in and finish him off. When the Gladiator attacked, however, the 'straggler' lost height and flew beneath the other four bombers. The Gladiator stuck to his tail and followed him, whereupon the bombers above opened fire with their downward-firing, movable guns. It was the 'lame dog' trick and by no means a new idea, but on this occasion it nearly put paid to the Gladiator, which was lucky to get away with only superficial damage. The pilot immediately passed on his knowledge to the rest of the Flight, who observed the same manoeuvre on subsequent raids that day but were able to avoid getting caught.

The Regia Aeronautica tried everything they knew to destroy Faith, Hope and Charity. The Three Graces would find themselves engaging, on raid after raid, day after day, formations of thirty or forty aircraft. CR 42s and Macchi 200s would come hunting for them in packs, but somehow the little biplanes outmanoeuvred them, slippery and elusive as fishes.

They found they could hold their own with the CR 42s, although they had to use all their skill to do so. The little Italian biplanes, so similar in many ways to the Gladiators themselves, were highly manoeuvrable, sturdy little aircraft. Both aircraft had machine-guns that fired between the blades of the revolving airscrew. But the types of interrupter gear used were very different. The system employed in the British machine was based on the action of an oil impulse, while the CR 42 used a complicated system of gears. The British gear was far more fallible. It only needed a tiny oil leak and the whole system might fail, with serious results. On the other hand, the Italian gear was much heavier, thus reducing the speed of the aircraft. Even so, the CR 42s were 10 miles an hour faster than the Gladiators and the British pilots treated them with great respect.

The Macchis, of course, were much faster than the Gladiators and the latter had to go very warily when these sleek monoplane fighters were in the air. On the whole, however, they gave them less trouble than the CR 42s. Although so much faster, the Macchis were not nearly as agile, and the Gladiator pilots found that they could, more often than not, outmanoeuvre them.

Aerobatically the Gladiators were superb. If ever an aircraft could be said, to use a threadbare phrase, to be able to 'turn on a sixpence', it was the Gladiator. This facility, plus their slow speed, enabled them, in the hands of their skilled pilots, to hold on in the sights of a fast-diving Macchi until the last minute, then turn quickly and deftly out of harm's way with a smart 'flick of the wrist' – the same trick practised deceitfully on Messerschmitt 109s by Swordfish.

Of course, it needed a skilled pilot, with courage and steady nerves, to do this. The men who flew Faith, Hope and Charity had the tremendous advantage of Royal Air Force training behind them. The rest they were well able to supply themselves, but their superior grounding in aviation they owed to the service whose reputation they were so steadily upholding. It was the matchless training that the Air Force gives to all its young aircrew trainees as a basic part, indeed a fundamental right, of their service.

The Gladiator pilots found that it was not difficult to out-think some of their less well-trained, less experienced counterparts in the Regia Aeronautica. A sudden reduction in speed, a sudden turn, often had an inexperienced 'bandit' tying himself in knots trying to keep on the British aircraft's tail. In his frantic haste to turn with the Gladiator and avoid overshooting, the Italian would very often stall his aircraft and go into a spin. Many Italian pilots used to put their aircraft deliberately into a spin by way of evasive action. They did not seem to realise that an aircraft caught in a spin is a very easy target for an attacker. His forward speed as he loses height is so slow, compared with that of the following aircraft, that the other can simply circle round him and pick his shots.

In another respect the low speed of the Gladiators was turned to good account. They were so slow that it was comparatively easy for them to attack the bombers in beam approaches and get in some really good, accurate deflection shots. This sort of careful aiming and firing is very difficult for a modern fast fighter.

Superior skill, then, sound, if older aircraft, courage and coolness kept the pilots alive and the air defence of Malta flying. The repair and maintenance crews, too, kept the Gladiators always in first-class shape to the full extent of their unrivalled skill.

They were more than pulling their weight now and had proved themselves over and over again to have been worth the initial struggle to get them into the air. Their very presence was a tremendous morale builder for everyone on the island and they were seriously interfering with Mussolini's plans for an easy victory in Malta as a prelude to a big push by his North African army. They threw his bomber pilots off their stroke and made them miss more times than they hit their targets, forcing them to bomb from greater and greater heights so that accuracy suffered and the fish in the sea immediately round the coast of Malta died in increasing numbers. In addition to that they almost certainly caused the Italian fighter pilots to lose a great deal of face in the eyes of their Luftwaffe opposite numbers, not to mention the harm done to the Fascists' own overblown self-esteem. This was a desperate battle and every little helped.

But they had only scored one confirmed victory. They felt this keenly. They were not only, they felt, letting down the Royal Air Force, to which they were all, within themselves, so proud to belong, as well as the thousands of Maltese people who trusted them so blindly, but they felt also that their lack of success reflected personally upon their own professional ability. There were good reasons in plenty why their scoreboard was almost blank, but to the pilots these were only excuses, and the names that crowned their aircraft only empty symbols reflecting ironically on their achievements to date.

It never rains but it pours, and now something else happened to add to their frustration. The extra boost they had been getting had made a big difference to the performance of their aircraft. But they knew it could not last for ever.

One morning, after a very heavy raid, the Gladiators landed, picked their way gingerly up the flight path between the packing cases and the buses and came to rest. Jock Martin climbed stiffly out of his cockpit and limped over to Nobby Clarke, who had come to see if there was anything in need of repair – there usually was.

'Lord, what a party,' said Jock. 'I damn nearly bought it this time. The boost's gone, can't get near 'em. A bloody big Macchi came and wiped my tail for me. I don't know what it is that's gone u.s. but she just hasn't got it any more – can't touch 'em. Can you get your chaps on to it as quick as you can?'

'We've been expecting that to happen for days,' said Nobby. 'Lucky to have lasted as long as they have. I'll get my section on to it right away.'

Yes, well, I hope you can get the old lady airborne again pretty smartly – they're corning over in bloody droves. And no more engines if this lot goes u.s., eh? Then we *are* up the creek!'

The expected had happened. The extra boost had begun to tell – on the engines. Then John Waters landed with the same sad story. Sergeant Dimmer and his men stripped the engine of Waters's aircraft and found a hole as big as a two-shilling piece in one of the cylinder heads. This was an emergency and there was no time to get the machine to Kalafrana, so they set to and did a quick repair job there and then on the airfield. By now another raid had developed and work on the engine had to be carried on at top speed in between dashes to the shelters, as bombs were falling on the airfield all the time, raising clouds of dust that choked the mechanics working in the open on the exposed Gladiator. There was no stopping for lunch this time – the job had to be finished in one stretch and as quickly as possible. Swiftly they removed the damaged component, then fitted a new cylinder and piston-rod and reassembled the engine. The Gladiator was ready to fight again.

Where had the spare cylinder and piston-rod come from? Once more the Engineers had come to the rescue. As soon as the Mercurys started cracking up they were told that they would have to think of something else in a hurry.

Once more Squadron Leader Louks had an idea. What about those Mercurys they were holding for the Blenheims? They might have a shot at converting them. The complications would be enormous but it was worth a try.

The job was one big headache from the start. The Gladiators were fitted with Bristol Mercury 8A engines, but the Mercurys at Kalafrana were quite different. Some of them were Mercury 8s, designed for short-nosed Bristol Blenheim twin-engined medium bombers, while the others were Mercury 15s, intended for the long-nosed version of the Blenheim. They were all very different in detail from the original Mercurys fitted to the Gladiators.

But they were manna from heaven to the Aircraft Repair Section. In fact, it was a cylinder and piston-rod from one of these Blenheim engines that went into Waters's aircraft to replace the punctured one. Then the real work of converting the Mercury 8s and 15s began.

The Blenheim engines were designed to operate all kinds of auxiliaries that would not be needed on the Gladiators and all these had to be sealed off before the engines could be fitted. Then the oil sumps, petrol pumps, carburettors and many other fittings were all very different. The mechanics had to change all these things, with insufficient technical knowledge of these particular engines. And they had to do it all at the double in the midst of air-raids.

Thanks to their determination and their skill as craftsmen, they managed it, and started to replace the worn-out engines with the new spare ones. But their troubles were not over. When they fitted the first replacement engine and tried to run it, oil started pouring out of the air intake. So they had to strip the whole engine down again and find out what they had done wrong. As it turned out, they had overlooked a little gadget called an oil-thrower ring, which the Gladiator engines had fitted to them but the Blenheim Mercurys did not. It was this small component that was holding them up.

Eventually, however, they persuaded the engine to run smoothly, it was flight-tested by the Command Engineer, Squadron Leader Louks himself, and found satisfactory. Faith, Hope and Charity took on a new lease of life – until the next thing went wrong.

In every respect the maintenance mechanics were doing a wonderful job, working twenty-four hours a day, and most of that under fire. They ate and slept at the job and did everything humanly possible to keep the Gladiators flying. Without them there would have been no 'Faith, Hope and Charity' at all.

Small wonder then that the pilots felt the ignominy of an almost blank scoreboard. Everything seemed to conspire to add to their frustration. The continual irritation of small accidents to the aircraft caused by having to land across wind on the narrow, fixed flight path, helped a great deal in this direction. The Operations Record Book reveals part of the story.

'21.6.40 PM: Gladiator crashed while taking off. Squadron Leader A. C. Martin uninjured.'

Uninjured, but considerably irritated and not a little shaken, a bad frame of mind in which to be taking on odds of forty to one in the air. Taking off or landing, these infuriating little mishaps were constantly occurring.

'PM: Gladiator collided with Queen Bee whilst landing. F/O Woods uninjured.'

Burges recorded four cases of engine failure during the first week of operations and seemed to be never free from the annoyance of minor mishaps. These were never very serious in themselves, merely oil leaks and things of that nature, but they were quite sufficient to put a pilot off his stroke in the air.

And it wasn't only the engines that were feeling the strain. For the first few days the pilots had split up into two flights, with three pilots on duty at a time and three off, changing every four hours. But as the number of raids increased and the days went on, the system of four hours on and four off from dawn (5am) until dusk (8pm) began to put much too heavy a strain upon them all, aircraft and pilots alike. The system was changed, therefore, so that only two men were on duty at a time, and each pair got one day off duty in every three. This new scheme came into operation towards the end of the first fortnight. It also saved a considerable amount of wear and tear on the machines, although, of course, it meant that normally only two machines would now be airborne at any one time instead of three.

They also made an important change in interception technique. Malta, like Britain, had radar, but the sort of warning system used in Britain, where there was time for the fighters to be vectored on to the German bombers after the first warning of the enemy's approach had been given, was impracticable on the little island. There, Control, on receipt of a warning from the Malta radar, would, at the time of the early raids, attempt to vector the Gladiators on to the target. But owing to the shortness of the distances involved and the Gladiators' slowness of climb, the bombers would be over the target and would have dropped from 15,000 or 20,000 feet to 10,000 feet before the slow fighters could reach them. This technique was now scrapped at the request of the pilots. Under the new system the radar merely gave the position of the enemy and no interception course was given. In fact, after the first day and his unsatisfactory experience in attempting to intercept the first SM 79s to appear, George Burges found himself taking very little notice of the Controller. The number of targets for the Italians was so limited that, amongst the few that there were, it was easy for the Gladiator pilots to anticipate the movements of the enemy bombers. They rapidly became used to Italian habits and began to know where to look for them almost by instinct. The radar, of which there was only one temperamental set perched somewhat precariously on the cliffs, was far from being 100 per cent effective. When the set was wrecked by a gale and was out of action for three days, it was not greatly missed.

Complementary to the new technique, Fighter Flight adopted a new scheme for scrambling. The old practice had been to stand by somewhere near the aircraft, as pilots did in Britain, then run to the machine when the alert sounded. This all took a lot of time, however, and the Gladiators needed all the time they could get if they were to climb above the invading bombers and dive on them when they came within range. So, once again, the old system was scrapped. Now, the pilots stayed in their cockpits throughout their period on duty, strapped in and ready for an immediate take-off when the warning sounded. It was calculated that this innovation gained for them a good 2,000 feet in height, which might mean the whole difference between catching the Italians and missing them altogether.

Mussolini's latest boast had been that he would be in Valetta in two weeks. These two weeks had now gone by and he was still in Rome. However, sticking to the schedule they had received, the Axis Radio announced: 'The Italian Air Force has completely destroyed the British Naval Base at Malta.'

Late on Saturday evening, 22 June, the radar reported a bogey approaching from the north.

At Hal Far, Burges and Timber Woods were on duty, strapped in their cockpits. They scrambled immediately and climbed flat out.

Their target was a single enemy bomber, an SM 79, which approached from the north of Grand Harbour and flew right down the island towards Kalafrana at about 13,000 feet. By the time the enemy machine had reached the centre of the island the two Gladiators were high enough to make their attack. They dived towards him. Later Burges submitted his report on the engagement. It was terse and to the point.

'Ordered to intercept enemy aircraft reported approaching Malta. Enemy sighted at 13,000 feet when we were at 12,000 feet. Altered course to intercept and climbed to 15,000 feet, and carried out stern attack from above enemy. Port engine and then starboard engine of enemy caught fire and attack was discontinued.'

The Italian aircraft had come over to take photographs of the 'destruction' of 'the British Naval Base at Malta' so blithely reported by the Axis Radio the night before, and had received its just and highly poetic desserts. It eventually fell into the sea off Delimara Point.

Evening promenaders in Valetta and along the Sliema waterfront were able to watch the whole satisfying spectacle. They saw the Italian bomber fall in flames and watched two of its crew bail out and follow it down by parachute. These two were the first Italians to set foot on Malta after hostilities had begun. But they came as prisoners.

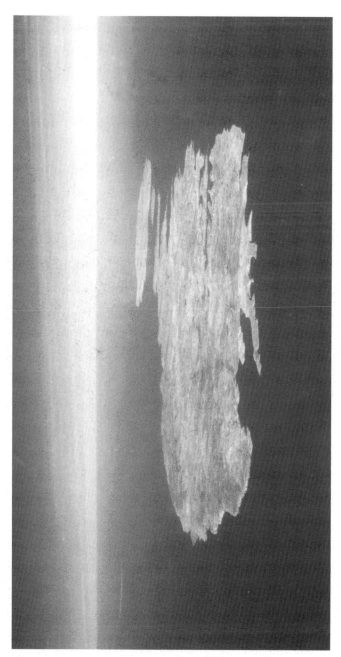

The island of Malta 'sits like a leaf on water' in this wartime photograph taken from an approaching aircraft on a clear day. *(Wise Owl Publications)*

Wing Commander George Burges,
OBE, DFC.

Wing Commander Peter Hartley.

Timber Woods, John Waters and Jock
Martin's dog.

F/O Collins in his role as Aerodrome
Defence Officer.

Taken before World War II, this is Fort St Angelo at the entrance to Grand Harbour in Malta with Royal Navy warships moored in line astern. It is apparent what an excellent target the area makes for air bombardment. (*via B Ketley*)

One of the most famous of the Sea Gladiators defending Malta is N5519, 'R', seen here at Hal Far in June-July 1940. Part of the Hal Far Fighter Flight, N5519 was known by the nickname 'Charity' and was shot down and lost on 29 July 1940, the RAF pilot, F/O P. W. Hartley being badly burned. *(via B Ketley)*

Sea Gladiator N5519 in true sea-going mode. Coded 'G6A' indicating 802 Naval Air Squadron, the aircraft is seen here landing aboard HMS Glorious sometime between June and September 1939. *(via B Ketley)*

Service divisions became blurred on Malta under the threat of constant bombardment. Here army troops are making up belts of ammunition for use by RAF aircraft. *(via B Ketley)*

Police assist in the clearing of rubble from blitzed buildings in Valletta.
(Wise Owl Publications)

War torn Valletta – Strada Reale (today Republic Street) after the deliberate
bombing of the capital city by the Luftwaffe on April 7th, 1942. The Royal Opera
House, a landmark at the city entrance, lies in ruins. It is still a gaping hole to date
as it was never re-built. *(Wise Owl Publications)*

A Fiat CR.42 at Wied Il-Ghajn. (*Wise Owl Publications*)

A graveyard for crashed aircraft. On the left is a fuselage belonging to one of the Gladiators. *(Wise Owl Publications)*

Gloster Sea Gladiator No 5531 burnt out at Hal Far after a direct hit on February 4, 1941. On the same day two other Sea Gladiators were damaged in combat. *(Wise Owl Publications)*

Hurricanes at Ta' Qali. The aircraft in the background is fitted with a tropical filter and has black/white undersides. *(Wise Owl Publications)*

CHAPTER FIVE

'We'll Fix It'

' **I** got into a lovely position where I just couldn't miss.'

Burges told his story of Faith, Hope and Charity's second confirmed victory with some excusable jubilation, although he was normally rather a serious young man, dedicated to a career in the Air Force and, in many ways, a typical product of Cranwell and the regular RAF.

His victory was a tribute to the work of a team, as well as to the skill and courage of one man. Their new tactics had worked and so had the new engines.

The Maltese were jubilant over the shooting down of the Italian aircraft, and Station Fighter Flight in their turn felt they had justified the confidence everyone at Hal Far had shown in them and the hard work that the mechanics from Kalafrana, with their army helpers, had put in to keep them flying. Whatever might have happened to lower their own confidence in themselves and their machines, this victory helped to restore. What they lacked in quantity they made up for in quality. That quality counts is a well-tried axiom that has saved Britain from disaster many times. Britain is the world expert at making a little go a long way.

On the 24th, two days after Burges's victory, the Prime Minister sent a prophetic message to the Governor of Malta. He said:

'The Cabinet watches with constant attention the resolute defence which your garrison and the people of Malta are making of the famous fortress and island. I have the conviction that you will make that defence glorious in British military history and also in the history of Malta itself.'

General Dobbie's reply reflected the spirit of Malta. He said:

> 'The garrison and people of Malta are fully
> determined with God's help, to maintain the integrity
> of this part of the British Empire, no matter what
> happens, and whether the time be long or short we
> have every confidence in final victory.'

Now began the heyday of Faith, Hope and Charity. Now they
had got their hand in, and the six men of Fighter Flight – Pete
Alexander had been posted to Gibraltar – threw themselves
into the fight with zest and determination renewed.

They began a run of victories. Shortly after Woods had
broken his duck, George Burges scored again.

'I got involved in a dog-fight just off Sliema with one of
the Macchis,' he said after the combat. 'It was real 1914-15
stuff, everybody chasing each other round. I managed to
shoot him down.'

By now British pilots and Italian had got to know each
other's ways fairly well, although both sides were of course
constantly evolving new tactics and manoeuvres in an effort
to get the upper hand. The Italians' respect for the three
infuriating Gladiators was considerable, behind the blatant
facade of the official party line, which daily perjured itself
and twisted truth into knots in a frantic attempt to make facts
fit the theories and justify the efforts of the Regia
Aeronautica to the Italian people and to Mussolini's
companion in crime. Although Italian bombing was good
enough to keep Malta's defences busy and her senior officers
worried, the accuracy of their bombing was hardly as good as
the mathematical correctness of their formation flying. In
fact, it seemed as if the Italian Air Force was a braggart with
an inferiority complex, looking to superior numbers and the
strict letter of formal military organisation to make up for the
individual enterprise they lacked.

Of course it is all too fatally easy to fall into such
generalisations about the characteristics of nations,

particularly in assessing their capabilities for waging war. All sides were guilty of such foolish platitudes, the attaching of vague labels that have been coming unstuck, ever since Napoleon called the British 'a nation of shopkeepers' and the Kaiser dismissed her 'contemptible little army'.

In such a way it is usual to deride the Italians as fighting men and dismiss their whole war effort, forgetting the Italian frogmen and those other brave men who fought a good war in spite of the dead hand of Fascism.

But the pilots who fought the Italians in the air over Malta learned a truer picture. There were some rabbits among the Italian airmen, but on the whole they were good fliers. The regular pilots especially were very good and their bombing formations immaculate, in the face of attack by fighters and anti-aircraft guns in heavier and heavier concentrations. 'The sort of thing you used to see at Hendon,' as Burges put it. The quality of the Italian fighter pilots seemed uneven. Some were very good and brave, others worthless. It is tempting to think that the best Fascists were the poorest pilots, but one pilot that Burges forced down in Malta after a truly epic dog-fight involving great skill and determination on both sides turned out to be, as he said, 'a very nasty bit of work, an out-and-out Fascist.'

The Italians were let down badly in the matter of their equipment. The good workmen among them had to suffer bad tools. Burges commented, after the siege of Malta was over: 'The trouble was, from their point of view, that only about half their bombs went off, and those that did went "pop" instead of "bang".'

Badly made, undersized bombs blunted their attack, and poor guns their defensive powers.

'I noticed,' said Burges, 'that whenever I went in at one, the trajectory of their tracers – they had those point-five guns – was very poor. Their armament was very bad altogether. With better bombs and better guns it might have been a different story. I'd blame the armament, not the individuals.'

That is the verdict of a man who should know, although it should be remembered that it is also the opinion of a modest man. It certainly does not detract from the achievements of Faith, Hope and Charity, especially when we learn that, in Burges's estimations, the average Italian pilot had more courage in the face of opposition than many of his Luftwaffe counterparts.

'I found,' he said, 'that the Germans were far more willing to break formation and leg it back home.'

He found too that most German fighter pilots had far less stomach for individual combat, man to man, than the pilots of the Macchis and CR 42s he met over Malta, usually preferring to remain in large packs at a great height, with occasional sorties to attack defenceless men, women and children on the inland roads of Malta or to pick off a wounded straggler in a damaged Hurricane or Spitfire. This is a technique they may well have learned from the inspiration of their chief, Hermann Göring, for this was the method by which the great Baron von Richthofen scored many of his swollen bag of victories over the German side of the western front in the First World War, when the future Reichsmarschall and Luftwaffe chief was a humble line pilot in Richthofen's staffel.

Burges himself had many exciting personal combats with Italian fighter pilots, as did most of the pilots of Fighter Flight. In particular, many individual dog-fights took place between the Gladiators and the CR 42s, but the Gladiators were nearly always a match for them and even the Macchis bothered them very little in the end.

The routine for the Gladiators, although vaguely standardised, was never quite the same twice running. About the only constant factor was the absolute necessity for scrambling with the utmost speed so as to be in a commanding position when the Italian bombers arrived over their target. The target itself was always either Hal Far or Grand Harbour – aircraft or ships. That much was easy

V

to anticipate. But getting to a suitable position above the enemy needed every possible economy in technique.

The detailed methods of scrambling varied considerably as fresh possibilities were tried out. The basic practice of having pilots ready and waiting, strapped into their cockpits, was not changed. The actual signal, however, which gave them the cue to get airborne, was constantly being altered in an effort to produce the most immediately effective response on the part of the pilots. Klaxon horns, Very lights, telephones, even an old hand bell, were all variously used from time to time.

It was always oven-hot out on the flight path. The pilots would sit there, strapped in, like condemned men on the electric chair before the switch is thrown. Jock Martin used to sport a gaily coloured parasol to keep the sun off. After a while most of them used to take a book with them and turn over the pages idly out there in the hot and cramped cockpit, getting pins and needles in the bottom, waiting for the inevitable signal that sent them roaring off down the narrow, twenty-yard strip of brown, burnt, oil grass.

When the signal came, be it horn, light, telephone or bell, book and parasol went overboard and in a few seconds engines were shuddering and bellowing into life. They were always kept warm, as there was no time for testing engines or any of the niceties of orthodox drill. Then they were off, tearing down the flight path, the tail came up and they were airborne, climbing steadily into the sun, one after the other. Then the R/T would start to crackle.

'Banjo [Hal Far] from Red One. Red One and Two airborne.'

'Red One from Banjo. Bandits approaching St Paul's Bay from north.'

'Banjo from Red One. Your message received and understood.'

A pause.

'Banjo from Red One. Angels fifteen over Hot Dog [Grand Harbour].'

'Red One from Banjo. Bandits closing St Paul's Bay.'

'Banjo from Red One. Your message received. Angels now eighteen over Kalafrana.'

'Red One from Banjo. Guns engaging bandits.'

'Red Two from Red One. Tally ho! Bandit two o'clock starboard! Going down to attack.'

There would be no R/T for the next minute or so as machine-guns chattered in the brilliant hollow of the sky. Then perhaps there would be a jubilant shout of 'Grand slam!' – if the victorious pilot remembered his R/T code in the heat of the moment. But it was far more likely to be just, 'Got the bastard!'

This sort of procedure never varied very much. First the hectic climb. Then position yourself in the sun and watch for the ack-ack bursts to show you the position of the enemy. Then the dive on to the target. It was of such a dive, with the wind in the wires and throttle wide open, that Burges said: 'It took the paint off my wingtips. I could see the paint peeling off the wings.'

After that – throttle back to sit on his tail and get in a quick burst as soon as possible.

In that blinding sunlight it was easy for the eye to be fooled. It was on this account that Burges always flew with his cockpit hood open. In the brilliant, empty expanse of pure blue sky, a tiny scratch on the Perspex of the hood could look, out of the corner of the eye, like an enemy aircraft in the distance. One day Burges chased a very elusive bandit all over the sky and almost back to Sicily when he discovered that the 'bandit' was a fly carrying out its own evasive action inside the cockpit.

So it went on, day after day in that hot June weather, with the tired machines and weary men taking off time and time again through the burning air after a nerve-racking wait out on the flight path, 'cracking like a leg of lamb in the oven', to face the same endless struggle of one against scores, with perhaps a flaming Macchi or CR 42 or SM 79 as a prize, to land finally with a shot-up engine or a shattered rudder through the dust and smoke of bombs. Even the battle damage of an obscured, crater-torn airstrip – only twenty yards wide anyway – or just plain fatigue, could result in a burst tyre on touching down, a wingtip scraped, or an airscrew bent.

If that happened the pilot was supremely unpopular. Never were they allowed to forget that they were few in number, men and machines, and that replacements were non-existent. The Command Engineer never ceased to remind them of the necessity for caution in the handling of the old machines. 'Don't use too much boost,' was the cardinal rule, and he drummed it into them before every scramble.

Every damaged cylinder, airscrew or aileron had to be repaired instantly and, in most cases, out on the open airfield with bombs falling all the time. The routine servicing of the Gladiators, the necessary boredom of inspection both before and after flying, and the replenishment of fuel, oil and ammunition, was carried out regularly and unflinchingly under almost constant fire by the service personnel of the airfield, any damage or repair required being reported at once to the Aircraft Repair Section.

If an aircraft came in damaged, repairs were begun at once and the work proceeded night and day without a break until the repair was complete. The system that the Aircraft Repair Section had worked out in theory before hostilities commenced turned out well in practice. Two or three of the aircraft would usually be airborne at the time of a raid, leaving at least one less heavily damaged machine on the ground. Then, if one of the machines returning from combat should have been seriously damaged, this one would be replaced if possible by the reserve aircraft. Mechanics would then go immediately to work to bring the damaged machine to a state of airworthiness again with all possible speed. Sometimes there were no serviceable aircraft in reserve at all. At these times everyone simply hoped against hope that the machines then up in the fight would come down unscathed or at least with only minor damage.

The men of Kalafrana never rested. From the very first day of raids the telephone from Hal Far rang almost incessantly with calls for repairs. The NCOs of the Aircraft Repair Section, their defence duties now coordinated by Flying Officer Collins, their Commanding Officer who was also now the Aerodrome Defence Officer, supervised the exceptionally skilled Maltese mechanics, and soon it was necessary to establish a light repair section on the airfield itself.

The service personnel worked always with their small arms beside them, ready for instant use in the event of a sea or airborne landing on the island. Work continued during alerts, but on an alarm being sounded one man from each detachment would take up position at a point of vantage, with a whistle between his teeth. If the whistle blew it meant 'every man for himself'. That this procedure worked was proved by the fact that there were no casualties among these men during the first sixteen months of the siege, although there were some very unpleasant moments. Civilian employees on the airfields became quite as used to the continual hazard as the servicemen.

As for working hours, for as long as a fighter remained unserviceable it was worked on to full capacity until it was serviceable again. Collins himself was on his feet twenty hours a day. Following their Commanding Officer's example the men of the Repair Section worked all out while work was required of them, then, at dusk each night, if not required for aircraft work, all service personnel took up defence positions, at one of the four sector headquarters, at a machine-gun post, a fire-fighting or first-aid post. Collins found the important job of Aerodrome Defence Officer onerous enough in itself, without mentioning his main and even more vital duties at Kalafrana. An inspection tour of the Station Defence line took him three hours.

Sometimes the appalling conditions of strain and fatigue were too much for the men working on the aircraft. Exacting work requiring precision and intense concentration under dangerous conditions all day, followed by nights of continual bombing, was more than the human physique could stand. A fitter working on the top of an aircraft's mainplane would tap on the wing in the normal way to attract the attention of the man working on his back on the undersurface of the wing, and get no response.

The normal extent of damage to the Gladiators was so great that the mechanics who had alone seen the full extent of it would marvel to see the repaired aircraft take to the air at all, let along go into combat against the Italian fighters and bombers.

'How he got that old kite to do a victory roll without something falling off beats me,' said one aircraftsman.

Some of the damage had to be seen to be believed. On three occasions a Gladiator landed with its tail unit almost shot away and hanging by a couple of spars and a scrap of wire. Another time an aileron was almost cut in two. In all cases, however, the aircraft had remained under control. This fact speaks wonders for the firm that had designed them, the men who repaired them and the skill of the pilots in bringing them back. It was no uncommon thing to find bullet holes all round the cockpit, through the centre section of the mainplane above the pilot's head and through the instrument panel in front of him.

The pilots were quick to express their gratitude for the priceless work of the Aircraft Repair Section. They knew they could always count on the quick return to serviceability of a damaged aircraft and were at all times completely confident in the work carried out. One or another of them would often call in at the section when some particularly tricky job was under way to see how the work was going.

After a landing with the aircraft badly shot up from a dog-fight, Flying Officer Collins would carry out an immediate inspection with the pilot hovering anxiously in the background, while this sort of conversation went on.

Pilot: 'You're looking worried, Mick. Can't you mend it?'
Collins: 'Well, look for yourself.'
Pilot: 'Crikey! And I actually *flew* with that shambles!'
Collins: 'Looks as though you've let the moth get into it.'
Pilot: 'It's those bloody explosive jobs. But you can manage

it, Mick, can't you? Never known you beaten yet. Can do?'

Collins: 'You know us. If it can be done, we can do it. If we can't do it – it just can't be done. Can't say any more than that.'

Pilot: 'Good old Mick. You'll think of something. You've never let us down yet.'

Collins: 'Don't worry, we'll fix it.'

And they always did. That is the highest tribute that can be paid to them, and to all the men who have helped to keep the aircraft of the Royal Air Force flying: Don't worry, we'll fix it.

In their off-duty hours the pilots found that there was still plenty of recreation to be had in Malta. On their days off they might go sailing or swim or just lie in the sun at Sliema of Ghaiu Tuffeia. Various clubs and pubs were open to them in Sliema or Valetta. There was the Moulin Rouge, and Auntie's and Rexford's in the Strada Stretta. There was Maxim's too, where the genial Tony Bottighi would present the lucky pilot with a bottle of champagne for every victory scored, a custom that unfortunately came to an end when Tony himself was arrested on a charge of black-market activities. Caruana's bar in Kingsway was another favourite. Here they could always be sure of sympathetic service at the hands of portly, florid Captain Caruana himself. Also in Valetta there was the Union Club, and in Sliema the Sliema Club. It was here, one boisterous evening, that a naval lieutenant drove his small two-seater Morris round the ballroom, for which original behaviour he was subsequently dismissed his ship by an Admiralty whose sense of humour was not equal to the occasion. Another riotous evening ended by 'Cully' Cullen, a rugger-playing tough from Australia, climbing the statue at Kalafrana and placing on the top the sort of unmentionable object that is so often placed on the heads of statues. There were many congenial places to relax in, many friends and hospitable hosts. But the best of them all perhaps was Felix – Felix, who would serve you a whole young fried chicken, cooked in wine, with chips, for five bob.

As the size of raids was stepped up and the battered Gladiators became more and more patched and battle-scarred, the need for caution increased. The longer their charmed life stretched, the less expendable they became. This led to the pilots being ordered categorically to avoid combat whenever the odds were obviously outrageously heavy. Of course the order was open to individual interpretation, but the pilots realised only too well the possible results of losing even one of their precious machines, and kept a cautious eye on the odds. It went against the grain to avoid combat, but if discretion won now and again, no one would dream of bringing their valour into question. With only two or three aircraft in action at any one time it was hopeless now to try to break the enemy formations before they dropped their bombs. The best they could do was simply to try and make each sortie as expensive for the raiders as possible, and take no chances themselves.

'Don't take on too much,' they were told. 'Better to break off and save your aircraft for another time when the chances may be better.'

And even if that lucky day came and a pilot found himself in a good position for a burst and saw his bullets strike home, the chances were that he would never see a victory confirmed. With only a small expanse of land beneath on which an aircraft could fall, many a victim of a Gladiator's guns must have fallen into the sea and left no trace.

To the uninitiated the sky seems a big place, but the pilot alone knows how small it can be in practice, as full of trickery and treachery as the sea. For a Malta pilot forty enemy bombers and fighters could fill it completely. He might, for a brief second, find himself in a perfect position for a quick burst. Pressing the firing button, if he had been accurate he would see his shots hit in a vital spot, then he must break off or have half a dozen fighters on his tail. There was no time to sit and stare then, and follow his victim down to mark his end. In that sky a pilot could not relax for a second. With the sun's rays flashing off its polished surface, a bandit could suddenly loom as big as a house before he was noticed.

'You had to see him before he saw you,' said one of the pilots, 'the instant he came into your field of vision – or it might be too late. And if you did surprise him and catch him, the best you could hope for was to sit behind him as long as you could with safety and give him all you had, trusting to luck that the crossfire from his pals missed you. Then, if you were lucky, you might see pieces of his tail fly off suddenly, then his rudder, his undercart would come down and the broken pieces would zoom back at you like little meteorites and flash past so close that you would duck your head instinctively. It was very exhilarating. Then it was time to move on to fresh fields and pastures new.'

By now June was drawing to a close. It seemed incredible to the weary pilots and groundcrews that less than a month had passed since their first operational scramble. In these short weeks they seemed to have lived through a lifetime. For a unit of three old aircraft operating in such impossible conditions it *was* a lifetime. It was a miracle that any of them were still flying at all, that any of the original handful were still alive. But they were still very much alive – wearier and about a hundred years older, but still as determined as ever to go up after the enemy as long as they and their wonderful punch-drunk old machines would last. What took perhaps the most out of them was not the actual fighting but the anxious minutes of waiting to scramble, the eternity of nerve-racking suspense and sweating, cramped discomfort before the signal came and they could throw off the nagging itch of anticipation and purge it all in action. But they were young and fit and they could take a lot more yet.

And at least they were no longer alone. Just before Burges scored his victory on the 22nd, he and the other duty pilot were given a job that relieved the monotony. They were ordered to act as fighter cover for a force of twelve naval Swordfish torpedo-bombers that were to be based on Malta.

This was a sign of the times. Malta, declared indefensible by so many, the island that was to have fallen in a day, was still in Allied hands. Not only that, she was defending herself so well that it was now considered a justifiable risk to give her some aircraft with which she could begin her main job – attack. The Swordfish were to operate from the island against enemy ports and shipping, working under the orders of the AOC. When the naval aircraft approached Malta it was fitting that they should be met and escorted in by the machines of that little, immortal force that had made their coming possible at all.

It fell out that on the day of the operation a bored pilot was looking out of the window of the mess at Hal Far. Suddenly, to his intense surprise, a naval officer appeared out of nowhere riding a motorcycle. He was smoking a pipe and wore a pair of gold wings on his sleeve.

'Hello, old boy,' said the RAF officer. 'Where have you sprung from?'

'Well, actually,' said the rider, with a nonchalance that only Dartmouth can produce, 'I've just come from North Africa.'

The story behind this is almost as salty as it sounds.

In May a squadron of twenty-four Swordfish had been under training at Hyères, in the south of France. As Mussolini's belligerent tendencies were seen to mature, half the squadron was formed into a striking force to operate under the orders of the French Navy when and if the Italians came into the war. Then, on 10 June, Italy declared war. Four days later nine of the British Swordfish, led by Lieutenant Commander G. C. Dickins, went into action with a bombing raid on Genoa. They were thus the first aircraft to drop bombs on Italian soil. The aircraft themselves were manned by instructors and their pupils, who benefited greatly from such a practical lesson. The bombs they used were French but they were delivered to the Italians with the authentic Nelson touch, having been secured with good pusser's spun-yarn before take-off.

Three days after this sortie, the squadron received a signal from the Admiralty to leave France, and next morning, 18 June, they took off in two formations and steered for the French naval air station at Bone on the Algerian coast. They had 430 miles to fly before they reached Bone, heavily laden as they were with an extra complement of maintenance ratings, one of whom remarked, as he surveyed the small armada, 'Christ, just like a travelling circus!'

The flight took them four hours and twenty minutes. There were no reserve tanks on the aircraft and they arrived at their destination with the proverbial spoonful of petrol in the tanks. At Bone they stopped for a much-needed rest, then split up into two sections: one, the training half of the squadron, was to return to England via Casablanca and Gibraltar, while the other, under the command of Lieutenant Commander F. D. Howie, flew by way of Medjez-el-Bab to Malta.

They were amused to see the two old Gladiators come out to meet them from the tiny island, but less amused when they saw what they had to land on. As they circled Hal Far, all they could make out was a large collection of assorted vehicles, from buses down to perambulators, interspersed with barrels, drums and boxes, completely obscuring the airfield. There was no sign of anywhere to land.

'We've got the wrong island,' said one observer. 'Have we got to land in that junk-yard?'

'Oh, I dare say I can find an odd corner somewhere,' said his pilot.

Eventually they simply landed where they could, in between the obstacles, overburdened as they were with passengers and spare gear. Thanks to skill and not a little luck, they got down, as someone said, 'without bending anything'.

It was then that one officer climbed down from his cockpit, disappeared underneath the fuselage and unstrapped the motor cycle he had brought all the way from the south of France. Dragging it out from beneath the aircraft he propped it upright, got astride it and gave the starter a kick. It started immediately and he roared gaily off, threading his way among the cars and packing-cases, in the vague direction of the station buildings.

The Swordfish lost no time in going into action. They were operating under the command of the RAF now, and the Operations Book records:

> '23.6.40 AM: …Anti-submarine patrols by Swordfish of Fleet Air Arm.'

They also began bombing targets in Sicily. The Operations Book begins to include such entries as:

> 'Fleet Air Arm raid on oil refinery and oil tanks at Augusta.'

Hal Far had suffered quite enough raids without possibility of reprisal. Now the Swordfish were able to take the scrap to Mussolini for a change. Shortly after the highly successful night raid on Augusta, they bombed Catania airfield, scoring a direct hit on the hangars. That meant a few less aircraft for the Gladiators to take on next day.

These early beginnings of Malta's power to strike were auspicious of greater strength to come. These Swordfish established a beachhead and held on, as the Gladiators had already done on another front, worrying the enemy and showing everybody just what air power could do if used with intelligence and determination. Their persistent and successful attacks throughout put the Italian efforts to shame. Now Malta, thanks to Faith, Hope and Charity, was attacking as well as defending.

Anything the naval aircraft could do at this stage to stop Italian supplies and reinforcements from reaching Mussolini's African ports was of vital importance. For the Italians were massing all along the North African coast in obvious preparation for an attack on Egypt and the Middle East. Tactically Malta had beaten Mussolini in the skies above the island. Now she began to justify her great historical reputation as a vital strategic weapon.

The naval maintenance ratings soon came to show the same disregard of danger and the same unflagging energy as their RAF and Maltese civilian counterparts. They were exposed to the same incessant danger on the ground, with bombs falling continually as they worked on the aircraft with the airstrip sometimes receiving as many as a hundred bomb hits a day. Some of the Swordfish themselves were old types, with no blind-flying instruments. None of them had any special search equipment fitted. This meant that, in the event of a suspected enemy ship or convoy being reported, the aircraft had to search for the target themselves before they could feel that their night's work had not gone for nothing. 'Rat hunts' the Navy called these groupings in the dark. One young pilot put the case for the Fleet Air Arm when he said:

> 'It's a curious job in a way. When we are sent out after a target it is usually a matter of two or three hours' anxiety about whether we shall find it, two or three minutes' over whether we shall hit it – and then a lot more anxiety about whether we shall get home again. But it all helps to keep you young and happy, doesn't it?'

The lack of ASV equipment resulted in one or two anti-climaxes. Once they followed up a report of fifteen enemy destroyers and cruisers, only to discover that they had been chasing the shadows of fifteen small islands. Another fruitless 'rat hunt' produced the laconic entry 'Brilliant dawn attack on wreck' in the Squadron Commander's log.

While the Swordfish carried the war to the enemy by night, the Gladiators continued to go up against all comers during the daylight hours. Each force was now able to help the other. Anything Faith, Hope and Charity could do during the day to keep the Italian bombers from blasting the flight path at Hal Far and gouging it with craters would help the Fleet Air Arm machines to continue taking off on their nocturnal raids against Mussolini, even though the narrow strip was usually 'distinctly bumpy' as one naval pilot put it.

In return the Swordfish bombed enemy aerodromes and kept down the numbers of enemy intruders.

The Three Graces were still fighting and there was no let-up for them, nor would there be for many more desperate weeks. But, on 28 June, after they had been operating for nearly three weeks, they received a consolation prize.

A raid had just finished and the two duty aircraft of Fighter Flight had that moment landed. The pilots were walking away from their machines when suddenly there was a roar overhead and four monoplanes came in low over the airfield, waggling their wings. Instinctively, the two men ducked for cover. Then, with a look of utter astonishment on their faces, they straightened up and said as one, 'My God! Hurricanes!'

CHAPTER SIX

The First to Go

The Hurricanes had come from North Africa, and their story was every bit as epic as that of the Swordfish.

The Flight was led by Flight Lieutenant 'Jock' Barber, a South African. Barber himself had had bad luck to start with. First of all he force-landed on a hillside. On inspecting his aircraft for damage, he found that the electrics working his fuel pumps had broken down and that the rough landing had broken his tailwheel. However, he managed to get a car battery from the local garage and some bits of old wire, then, as he said, 'With an old car spring for a tail skid, I patched up the aircraft and took off for Tunis, just missing an HT cable. From there I hopped across to Malta.'

Malta was only intended to be a stepping-stone for these machines, on their way to the Middle East. Aircraft from various points of the compass habitually used the island as a refuelling stop and a transit base. Normally they were allowed to proceed about their lawful business unmolested. But this was different. These were *Hurricanes*.

Air Commodore Maynard seized his opportunity. Once again he worked a minor miracle and managed to persuade the Air Ministry to let him keep the four Hurricanes as part of his fighter force.

So the strength of the little unit was pushed up – by four. Together Gladiators and Hurricanes carried on the fight.

Burges was now the 'ace' of Fighter Flight, with six confirmed victories. On Saturday 13 July the *Times* of Malta ran a picture of Burges, and announced:

> 'His Majesty the King is graciously pleased to award the Distinguished Flying Cross to Flight Lieutenant George Burges for gallantry and devotion to duty in the air defence of Malta.'

The picture, cut from the newspaper, found its way into picture frames and windows all over Malta. Old people treasured the pilot's picture and prayed for him and his fellow flyers. Young girls stuck their new pin-up on the wall next to their beds. The Maltese coined a name for Burges. They called him '*Il Ferocio*'.

On their first raid after the arrival of the Hurricanes the Italians had yet another unpleasant shock. As well as the three devils they knew falling on them out of the sky, the bright sunshine disclosed four new, rather more lethal opponents. They began to realise that the RAF had really come to stay.

The immediate result of the British reinforcements was a stepping up in the Italian effort. Now the enemy began sending over extra-heavy fighter patrols, with whole flights of fighters stacked up in echelon hunting for the hard-pressed Malta defenders. The Gladiators and Hurricanes were kept busy fighting for their lives and the pace grew very hot indeed.

But they continued to score victories. The veterans, as they were by now, of the Battle of Malta tried their hand with the Hurricanes and produced some excellent results in the shape of damaged and destroyed enemy aircraft.

The incidence of damage to the British aircraft also increased sharply as a result of the increased pressure by the enemy. On the day on which the award of Burges's DFC was announced in the *Times* of Malta, only one Gladiator and one Hurricane were serviceable. These two took to the air and engaged the enemy as usual all day. In one combat the two aircraft became involved in a dog-fight with twelve of the highly manoeuvrable CR 42s and the Hurricane was badly damaged. The Italians increased their effort even further when they realised the dwindling strength of the Royal Air Force. The Regia Aeronautica made an all-out attempt to wipe out the enfeebled and seriously reduced Fighter Flight. But the mechanics outdid themselves at Hal Far and endeavoured to put three or four aircraft always in the air to meet each raid. Meanwhile the enemy tried everything he knew both by heavy fighter attacks in the air and by fierce assaults on their airfields, to smash the British fighters.

But still by day Gladiators and Hurricanes survived to take the air, while by night the Swordfish took off to strike Mussolini's ports and his ships at sea.

The pilots of Fighter Flight, who had long since grown used to the top-heavy odds against them, seemed indifferent to the new increase in numbers. Burges and Waters continued their interminable chess battle, while Jock Martin appeared to be far more worried about the health of his pet, a Maltese bull-terrier, than the Italians. Peter Hartley, who had established the nucleus of his small farm at Hal Far, went on tending his beloved pigs and chickens and was only observed to show any signs of agitation when any of the bombs fell too close to the animals. The 'farm' was now flourishing. In fact, it was going so well that Hartley's CO, the fiery-tempered 'Ginger' O'Sullivan, who had shown great interest in the experiments himself, began to complain that he was being unfairly treated.

'Look here, I'm the CO, it's my farm,' he said. 'You've cut me out.'

Timber Woods remained his calm, controlled self, although the occasional anti-cyclone of Celtic temperament was known to disturb the air. As these bursts of fire were usually vented, with telling effect, upon the unfortunate Italians, no one was worried.

Then the affairs of the Station struck a sour note. Jock's bull-terrier, of which he was so very fond, got in the way of a revolving airscrew. The whirling blades took away almost all the poor animal's face, and Jock, with Peter Hartley and one or two of the others, was forced to destroy her. They put her to sleep with ether. It was a long, unpleasant and painful business, as the dog was strong and fought for life. It was over at last, but the incident cast a small shadow of gloom over them.

Then things returned to normal as the pilots became absorbed once more in the serious business of working and playing hard.

Only in Peter Keeble did a marked change occur, and that had no relation to the rigours of the Malta blitz.

One day Burges came into the mess whistling as usual 'Here we go round the mulberry bush', and found a shocked-looking Keeble reading a letter.

'Hello, Peter,' said Burges sympathetically. 'Not bad new, I hope?'

'I'm afraid it is bad news, George,' said Keeble. 'My brother's been shot down – killed.'

Burges said all one can ever say in such a situation.

'I'm sorry, Peter,' he said. 'I'm damned sorry. It's rotten luck.'

'Well, that's the way it goes, I suppose,' said Keeble, though the hard glint in his eye said something else.

'George,' he said, 'I want to get one of those bastards today.'

'Yes, well, you take it easy up there,' Burges replied. 'Don't go trailing your coat.'

Soon after that the sirens went for a raid, the first of the day.

'Come on!' shouted Keeble from the cockpit of his Hurricane. 'What are we waiting for? Let's go and play games with the Eyeties!'

Burges looked anxiously across at him, remembering the bad news he had received that morning and the impression it had obviously made upon Keeble's impulsive nature. Then they were off and climbing to gain height.

As soon as they dived on to the enemy they found themselves involved with a mixed bag of Macchis and CR 42s. They went hard at it for a few minutes, each side trying to get one of their opponents in the sights. Then, suddenly, Keeble's excited voice came over the R/T.

'Red One from Red Two,' he shouted. 'This one's mine. Tally ho!'

There was silence over the R/T for a moment. Then a voice, low and angry, was heard to mutter, 'Right, you bastard, right!' Then machine-guns opened up.

But Keeble did not see the two CR 42s that, agile and wicked as snakes, had fastened themselves on his tail.

Burges shouted, 'Look out behind you, Red Two!'

Then Keeble saw them. He turned steeply to port to try and shake them off. But the CR 42s, though slower than the Hurricane, were more than a match for the British aircraft in manoeuvrability. He could not shake them off. He tried every trick he knew but they still stayed on his tail, hanging on like leeches. Keeble tried diving, throttle wide open, in the hope of losing the Italians, but when he levelled out the biplanes were still there.

By now they were over Grand Harbour and flying very low. In a last desperate attempt to elude the enemy, one of whom was very close behind him and obviously on the point of opening fire, Keeble led them down beneath the Pinella wireless masts in the hope that they would hit one of the aerials. But the trap failed.

As the two aircraft shot out from underneath the aerials the Italian gave the Hurricane a quick burst. Watchers below saw the bullets go home, creeping rapidly along the fuselage towards the old cockpit. Then, suddenly, the Hurricane gave a lurch and dived straight into the ground, where it exploded in a splash of bright flame. A second after the Hurricane had blown up, the CR 42 followed him, flying straight into the ground and blowing up instantly.

A gunner officer who had watched this combat between the two brave, skilled pilots, later said:

> 'I watched them turning and diving, trying to get a shot in at each other. That Italian was good, one of the rare ones, and he finally managed to get on Keeble's tail and shoot him down. He was so close to the ground when he fired at Keeble's plane that he couldn't pull out in time and crashed into the ground. They both fell in the same field within a few yards of one another. They were both very young men.'

So passed the first of the original few to die. Dashing, ambitious, good-looking and full of life, Peter Keeble had longed passionately to become an 'ace'. Perhaps he strove too hard. Impatient to succeed, hot-headed, he lacked the coolness in action, the ruthless concentration of a Bader or a Johnston. When the news of his brother's death came, his rage against the enemy, instead of making him more coldly ruthless, more concentrated and calculated in the task of killing the enemy, filled him instead with blind rage and a wildness to avenge.

His death came as a shock to everyone at Hal Far. Normally such a death in action, though mourned by friends at the time, quickly becomes an accepted fact in the turmoil of war. But the astounding immunity of the little squadron through six weeks of bitter fighting against outrageous odds had lulled everyone into a false sense of security, so that the original six pilots had seemed almost invulnerable.

Now they were only five. The heavy odds had told at last. Keeble fell on 16 July, taking his victor with him. Altogether on that day ten Italian aircraft were shot down over Malta and their pilots killed. It was, for both sides, a sad day to remember. In two messes there would be the odd, somehow unbelievable phenomenon of empty seats.

By now, British and Italian pilots had learned to respect each other. In fact, there had developed some slight reflection of the spirit which had existed on certain sectors of the Western Front in the 1914-18 war between some British and German squadrons. This showed itself in an incident that occurred during the Italian blitz on the island.

One day a CR 42 flew low over Hal Far and dropped a small canister suspended from a tiny red silk parachute. When it was opened the canister was found to contain a large, rolled-up cartoon. The cartoon depicted a CR 42 fighter. From the cockpit of the aeroplane projected a huge naked body with a big ace of spades painted on his chest. Swarms of British aircraft were depicted attacking the Italian fighter from all directions, while the Italian fighter was shown grabbing one RAF pilot by the neck with one hand and shattering another British aircraft with the other. Up in the top left-hand corner of the drawing, above a bunch of cumulus cloud, St Peter was shown sitting behind a booking-office desk, while a long queue of miserable-looking little RAF pilots, all wearing small heavenly wings, waited with their money in their hand for admission. On the back of the cartoon in Latin they read the following:

'Good morning and good luck to the boys of Hal Far and Kalafrana.'

The 'boys' needed all the good luck they could get. They certainly got no rest, especially the toiling men of the Aircraft Repair Section. Five weeks had now passed since Mussolini had first attacked the island. Repairs to the battered Gladiators were now more urgent than ever, and the Hurricanes had added a new load of responsibility to the backs of Flying Officer Collins and his men.

On one occasion a spare tail assembly was made up from bits and pieces so as to be ready to replace any damaged tail unit that a shot-up fighter might bring in. Many other such spare assemblies were more than ever the order of the day. The use of explosive bullets by the enemy caused frequent and extensive damage of a kind that could only be repaired by replacing the component.

Luckily the basic structure of the Gladiator, which was of tubular metal framework with wood fairings and fabric covering, lent itself to rapid repair work. Only once did a hold-up threaten to occur. In the tail of the Gladiator there was a tubular transverse member of quite a large diameter. A badly damaged Gladiator landed with two-thirds of this particular member shot away by explosive bullets. At first nothing could be found to replace the damaged component. To turn up one from solid metal would have taken much too long. Then, when everyone had just about written off the job as hopeless, Collins spotted the gun-flash tube on a damaged

Hurricane standing nearby. Calipers in hand, he rushed to the other aircraft. The outside diameter of the tube was exactly right, although the gauge of the metal was much too thin. The tube was taken off the Hurricane and Collins had the thin cylinder stiffened by the insertion of a hardwood plug. Another aircraft had been made serviceable.

'Reminds me of the days of wooden aircraft and iron men,' he said.

On another occasion a large formation of CR 42s was engaged by a Hurricane and a Gladiator. Collins watched them as they came in to land after the combat.

'See that aircraft?' he said. 'That's Gladiator by Hurricane out of Swordfish.'

Some of the men referred to this machine from that time on as the 'Gladfish'.

At one time the fighter force was reduced to one Hurricane and two Gladiators, leaving the Repair Section working frantically on the remaining machines in an attempt to bring them to serviceability. Somehow they got the necessary replacement parts made, but Collins had to put a stop to the story, which became famous round the aerodrome, that the McDonald bedsteads that had unaccountably disappeared froth the workshop hangar had been incorporated into the rejuvenated aircraft. The beds had in fact been used by the fire-fighting party, which rather spoiled a good story.

The struggle went on through the hot summer days, then, on the last day of July, Fighter Flight suffered another disaster.

Peter Hartley was a quiet, rather slow-speaking man, his heart as much in his farming as in flying. Like the others, he had been somewhat shaken by Peter Keeble's death, but it never occurred to him that anything like that could ever happen to him.

On the morning of the 31st he was leading a section of three aircraft. He himself had chosen the best of the Gladiators and, with Timber Woods and Flying Officer Eric Taylor, one of the Hurricane pilots and another farming enthusiast, behind him, was climbing flat-out in an attempt to reach the enemy formations. They were over Grand Harbour and closing in on one formation of bombers when they suddenly found themselves under attack by a swarm of diving Italian fighters that had jumped them out of the sun. Everyone started firing and a CR 42 dived on Hartley, firing rapid bursts. One of his bullets, an incendiary, hit Hartley's main petrol tank.

Instantly the cockpit was a hell of flame. The big 80-gallon, non-self-sealing tank, located right in front of the pilot, burst all over him, clad as he was in thin khaki drill, in a deluge of burning petrol. In a split second his body, crazy with pain, screamed out to him to jump. In that split second of terrible pain and fear his mind found time to register the thought, 'I'd jump even without a parachute.' Then he went over the side.

He was picked up, barely alive and terribly burned from head to foot, and taken in Imtarfa Hospital. When Burges went later to visit him there he was appalled by the extent of Hartley's injuries, and was convinced that the wounded pilot could not possibly live. In that he was to be proved wrong. Thanks to his own basic fitness and will to survive, and to the untiring efforts of a nursing sister in the hospital, Hartley recovered.

He was helped in his struggle back to health and fitness by frequent visits from friends. On one occasion some of the other pilots came to see him, bringing the Governor's young and attractive daughter, Maureen Dobbie, with them. Maureen was very much the bright young thing.

'Hello, Peter,' she said, looking at his heavily bandaged form. 'I hear you fell out of your aeroplane.'

This remark probably did as much as anything to put him on his way to recovery.

Another friend who really helped a great deal to restore Peter's badly damaged body was his crony Dr Freddie Moore. It was Moore who accompanied him in the ambulance to the hospital, who fought the Army doctors tooth and nail until his friend was given a private ward. And Freddie went on fighting them. His speciality was plastic surgery, of which his friend was now in such urgent need, and he battled with everything he knew against Army red tape in an effort to persuade the hospital authorities to let him try his own methods in the treatment of Hartley's burned body. At last, after an effort which would have moved mountains, if not the Army, he was grudgingly permitted to work on Hartley's hands only. When, eventually, the patient was pronounced fit, it was clearly observed that his hands were by far the most perfectly restored of all.

So Peter Hartley lived, and lived, what is more, to fight another day. When he was discharged from the hospital, he was posted home, much against his will.

'I was livid to have to go,' he said.

From then on his was a story of bitter struggle to get back into the air at the controls of a fighter. Many people in England told him he would never fly again. He was off flying for two years after the accident, having been declared unfit on his medical report. Then he managed to get himself posted to a Spitfire wing at Uxbridge, where he was given a flight. Then, much to his delight, the squadron was posted abroad. Hartley kept his fingers crossed, but everything seemed to be going well. His flying was not what it had been – yet. He knew he wasn't right but felt sure that practice would make him perfect and hoped that nothing would intervene to stop him from going abroad with the squadron. Eventually they got as far as Euston. Then, just as they were about to board the train, they were told that the boat was not ready, and sent back to Uxbridge. Once again they received orders to leave. On the day before they were due to leave Uxbridge Hartley went over to see his young brother, who was at that time training for the Air Force. When he returned to the station he found, to his bitter disappointment, that an order had come through to the effect that Hartley was not to accompany the squadron abroad. But he was not beaten. He went to Debden to try and convince himself and everybody else that there was nothing wrong with his flying. But he found that he still could not quite make the grade.

'I just couldn't do it, I couldn't do it,' he said.

Then he went to the Spitfire Officers Training Unit at Heston. By the end of the course he felt that he was ready at last to go on active service again. Having passed with ease, he was given command of the famous No 54 Squadron, which was at that time on rest in the north of England. He was still a little unsure of himself in the air. As he said himself later, 'I wasn't brilliant, but I led them and so on, and did all the things that were expected of me.'

Then he was posted to the Middle East with a Spitfire wing. He was given a squadron in the desert at El Alamein. In the desert he flew 'tank-buster' Hurricanes armed with cannon.

It was now that he began to see the truth of his medical report. Reluctantly he forced himself to admit that he was really unfit for active duty with the squadron. He gave in at last to the doctors, and was given Wing Commander's rank and an administrative job with No 241 Wing at Beirut. His flying days were over. But when he thought about it, he found that he had no real regrets. Truly, he had done enough.

CHAPTER SEVEN

Faith, Hope and Hurricanes

The main effort of the Malta Gladiators was over, although the survivors were to fight on for some months yet, as were the remaining Gladiators in other theatres of war. In the Battle of Britain a Gladiator squadron was stationed at Roborough to protect the Royal Naval Dockyard at Devonport. This was 247 Squadron, the last Gladiator squadron to operate in Britain.

Hopes in Malta were now based on an early delivery of more Hurricanes. The enemy was continually stepping up his fighter attacks on the meagre number of defenders. Whole squadrons of CR 42s would patrol the island now in the hope of luring the three or four British fighters to destruction against impossible odds. The Hurricanes and Gladiators treated such large formations warily, although their score continued to mount. It was no uncommon thing now to see two or more Italian machines falling in flames at the same time.

Air Commodore Maynard had made repeated requests for more fighters. At last, after Faith, Hope and Charity and the first Hurricanes had proved the practicability of defending Malta from the air, the Air Ministry decided to establish a proper fighter defence on the island. In spite of the very urgent need for fighters in Great Britain, a reinforcement of Hurricanes was ordered to Malta.

On 31 July, the day on which Peter Hartley was shot down over Grand Harbour, a convoy sailed from Gibraltar. The convoy bristled with warships. There was the aircraft carrier *Ark Royal*, two battleships, *Valiant* and *Resolution*, two cruisers, *Enterprise* and *Arethusa*, and a screening force of twelve destroyers. The valuable prize package that these ships guarded was the small aircraft carrier *Argus*, for she carried twelve Hurricanes bound for Malta.

The operation had really begun on 18 July, when a number of RAF officers assembled at Uxbridge. They had no idea where they were bound or what the mysterious job was to be. They were to be designated No 418 Flight, but beyond that anyone's guess was as good as another's. But many of them discovered that they had met before, that they had in fact flown together aboard aircraft carriers when the Air Force had manned the Fleet squadrons. This was highly significant and they drew the obvious conclusion. Next day they travelled by train to Abbotsinch and on the 20th began practice-flying on Hurricanes. This was nothing much more than flight-testing the machines, as they were familiar with Hurricanes and most of them were experienced in carrier work – always supposing that this job involved what they had guessed.

They were right. The same day they and their aircraft were embarked aboard the aircraft carrier *Argus*, then lying in Govan dry dock. The following day *Argus* left Govan and steamed up the Clyde to Greenock. Three days later she sailed with an escort at half-past six in the evening. The passage to Gibraltar took six days. They arrived there early in the morning, and immediately stores and maintenance mechanics for the Hurricanes were embarked in the submarines *Proteus* and *Pandora*, to creep into Malta through the minefields. The day after, the main force sailed for Malta.

When they were clear of Gibraltar the pilots were called together and given a briefing for their mission. They were to fly their aircraft off the carrier and deliver them to Malta. Having safely delivered them, they themselves were to be flown back to Gibraltar by flying boat. Because of their past experience of flying aircraft from carriers they were to act as special ferry pilots and take Malta the first of the fighters she had been crying out for. Shortly after this the ships were attacked by Italian bombers, but no damage was done.

They flew off *Argus* at a point 80 miles west of La Gelite. They had expected trouble on the take-off. The *Argus* was an old carrier, with a very small flight deck, and this was the first time she had operated modern aircraft like the Hurricane. They took the precaution of pulling out their boost plugs before take-off to make sure that they would have enough speed over the short deck to get their machines into the air. But it turned out to be unnecessary, and in the event none of them used full throttle. The Hurricanes went off the deck like birds and flew into the sunrise.

When they were airborne they split up into two flights of six, each flight attaching itself to one of the two Skuas detailed to escort them to Malta. After a flight of two and a half hours they caught sight of the island, looking, as one Flight Lieutenant put it, 'like a little white knob in a golden sea'. Shortly afterwards they landed at Luqa, just two hours and fifty minutes after they had taken off from the *Argus*. To say that they were welcomed with open arms would be to understate the case severely.

The following morning they met Air Commodore Maynard. They were all keen to know when the expected Sunderland would be available to fly them back to Gibraltar. They asked the AOC when they would be leaving.

'That's easy,' he said. 'You're not.'

Maynard had the reputation by now of keeping anything that came into his hands that might increase the effort of his tiny fighter force. Once again he had worked the miracle.

'No,' he said, 'I'm afraid you won't be catching the Sunderland. You'll be staying on here to fly the Hurricanes. What good are twelve fighters to me without the pilots?'

And that was that. They had no tropical kit and were totally unprepared for the Mediterranean, but they would just have to grin and bear it. One pilot wrote in his log book:

'3.8.40. Met AOC and heard awful news that we are to stay.'

This officer had made an appointment to meet his wife in England a few hours after his expected return from Malta. As it turned out he did not see her for five years. After being retained in Malta, where he played a distinguished part in the air defence, he was posted away from the island and subsequently taken prisoner. When husband and wife finally did meet, she said, 'You're a bit late, darling.'

The immediate reaction of the enemy to the new reinforcements was to send over a large force of fighters in an attempt to entice the newcomers into combat before they were blooded. But the odds were overwhelming and the offer was declined with thanks and deferred until a later date. Luqa, which was now being used by the Hurricanes, was heavily attacked in a vain attempt to put the only Malta airfield with runways out of action. Demonstrations in force by the Italians continued, although they took good care to remain at a respectable height.

The new pilots found themselves with their hands full of fighting. Losses began to mount up again. On 6 August two sergeant pilots wrecked their Hurricanes, and on the 15th another sergeant pilot was shot down and killed and his aircraft destroyed. Five days later one of the senior pilots of what was now 261 Squadron recorded in his log:

'20.8.40. Heavy air raid on Luqa. Transit Blenheim destroyed.'

These raids continued at all times of the day. The same pilot records later:

'29.8.40. Heavy raid on Luqa before breakfast.'

In September the pressure increased. The same log book reads:

'2.9.40. Seven scrambles. Record height 28,000 feet.'

Then, nine days later, he wrote:

'11.9.40. First Germans – Ju 87s.'

A new weapon had appeared – the dreaded Ju 87 or 'Stuka'. These German 'terror bombers', with which the Luftwaffe had had so much success in Scandinavia and the Low Countries, were not flown by Germans, however. They had been given to the Regia Aeronautica to help them carry out the Italian part of the Axis bargain and were manned by Italian air crews. Like their predecessors they made for the airfields. We read:

'17.9.40. Dive-bombing attack on Luqa.'

To the fury of its attack, the Stuka added a nerve-shattering scream. These Italian-manned Stukas, nicknamed 'Pichiatelli', had some success for a while but the British pilots soon discovered that the German machine was very vulnerable to fighters, especially when it had pulled out of its vertical dive, just after delivering its single heavy bomb. The Pichiatelli began to lose aircraft.

'87s were the easiest things on God's earth to push into the drink,' said one pilot. 'Just one squirt and it was over.'

15 September was a great day in the Battle of Britain, when the Luftwaffe suffered severely at the hands of Fighter Command. On that day twenty Stukas came over Malta, escorted by a large number of fighters, and delivered a concentrated attack on Hal Far, to try and put it out of action. Bombs saturated the airfield, and many delayed-action missiles were dropped, but the attack failed to prevent either the fighters taking off by day or the Naval Swordfish from 'rat hunting' at night, thanks largely to the ceaseless efforts of everybody on the airfield to repair the damage. On the 27th, the Flight Lieutenant commanding 261 Squadron spent an unquiet weekend. He wrote in his log:

'27.9.40. Took over command Luqa for weekend. Bombed to hell. Spent most of night repairing damage to runways.'

Somehow they always managed to repair them, although the Swordfish had an uncomfortable time of it taking off over the bumpy surface of Hal Far at night. But for 261 Squadron, worse was to come. A sombre entry occurs in the CO's log book:

'13.10.40. All taxis stopped.'

This was a serious blow. However, there was still the Archbishop's car. This was an old American car, once the property of the Archbishop of Gozo, which had been camouflaged and put into use as the Squadron car. In this old but excellent vehicle, the pilots of 261 would roar down the stone-walled roads of the island, pleasure-bent. Very often it took them to Dragonara Palace, the beautiful home of the Marquis Scicluna built out on a lovely promontory overlooking the sea, where they had a standing invitation and were always welcome. To leave the dust and dirt and danger of Luqa and drive to Dragonara was to escape into a brilliant, exotic world, where they were entertained like mythical heroes from a land of noble adventure, where the Marquis even kept a camel for the amusement of the children who ran laughing through the corridors of the Palace.

September was a busy and significant month for Malta in many ways. The advent of the Stukas turned out in the end to be merely a shadow of forthcoming events, though no one knew that the worst was yet to come. About this time, too, the Italians began to come over at night, to try and prevent repair work on the airfields and stop the Swordfish from operating, as well as carrying out their normal aim of destroying airfields and aircraft, which they thus did with less danger to themselves. To counter this new threat a small night-fighter force was organised by the RAF and from its inception began to have great success.

To balance the scales a little during this month, two big convoys arrived in Grand Harbour bringing precious food for the besieged, fuel for the aircraft and ammunition for the guns. The anti-aircraft defence of the island had been short of shells for some time, and the barrage increased noticeably in ferocity after the arrival of the convoys. As one officer wrote:

'The gunners had been waiting their chance and they took it with both hands, so much so that it was calculated that the stocks of ammunition in Malta would only last thirty days at that intensity of firing.

However, the Italians lost their enthusiasm and the ammunition situation unproved.'

The two convoys had been part of a big and very delicately balanced operation. To improve the situation in the Mediterranean and increase the power of British air resistance there, four ships were being sent out, the battleship *Valiant*, the anti-aircraft cruisers *Calcutta* and *Coventry* and, most important of all, the aircraft carrier *Illustrious*, a new ship and the first carrier to have an armoured flight deck. These ships came through the Mediterranean from Gibraltar between 30 August and 5 September. They were escorted as far as Sardinia by Admiral Somerville's Force H from Gibraltar, and south of Sicily the Battle Fleet met them and escorted them back to Alexandria. The passage of two fleets covering the whole length of the Mediterranean was too good an opportunity to miss. Each escorting force brought with it merchant ships loaded with supplies for Malta and managed to get them there safely, although the SS *Cornwall* arrived two days after the others, steering on main engines and with a gaping hole below her waterline.

On 23 October another brainchild of Squadron Leader Louks took its first steps. This idea was an attempt to cope with the Stukas. The pilots had found out that the Stuka was comparatively easy meat just after it had pulled out of its dive, when it was not yet under proper control, and the Command Engineer had the brainwave of adapting one of the surviving Gladiators as a special low-level fighter that could lie in wait for the Pichiatelli and knock them down as they floundered, weak and wobbly, after the exertion of their wild dive.

There was only one serviceable Gladiator left now. This aircraft continued to go up and fight alongside the Hurricanes, and was still priceless to the heavily outnumbered defenders. So this machine was definitely not available for experiments. However, there was one other Gladiator, crippled from continuous damage both in the air and on the ground, which had been written off as unserviceable. Louks took this machine and had it patched up. He took a more efficient propeller from another unserviceable machine and fitted it to the Gladiator. Then he improved the armament. The four machine-guns of the Gladiator had never really supplied enough fire power. If this machine was to shoot down Stukas he would have to increase its gun power. He did this by mounting two additional guns on the top wing, Great War fashion. When these modifications were finally complete the old Gladiator really looked like something from the old Western Front, as if Mannock or Ball or Bishop had flown in to help the Hurricanes of Malta. Looking at it in the half light of evening out on the grass in front of the hangar, with its biplane wings and guns mounted on the top plane, it looked a bit like a cross between a Nieuport Scout and an SE 5A.

It was certainly a hybrid, and someone, catching sight of it for the first time, re-christened it 'The Bloodiator'. Louks flight-tested the Bloodiator himself. The Command Engineer always tried to flight-test his machines personally. All engineers in the Navy and RAF are referred to as 'plumbers'.

'Well, I'm the *flying* plumber,' said Louks, and was proud of it. The Flying Plumber he remained.

By now the Italians had certainly lost some of their enthusiasm, and their bombing began to worry the Maltese population less and less.

In the comparative lull that now fell upon the island the authorities took the chance to set up a new and more workable organisation to coordinate the service and civilian populations, and to overhaul all the various sections of the island's defences. In England and Alexandria the Malta Shipping Committee was formed with the object of ensuring supplies to the beleaguered island, and on Malta itself the recruiting and training of men for the land defences was increased and intensified.

In September, too, had begun another aspect of Malta's vital part in the Mediterranean war. A number of Martin

Maryland aircraft arrived for reconnaissance work. These aircraft were put into action at once and began searching the skies over Italy, Sicily and Tripolitania on the lookout, mainly, for shipping, with occasional visits to enemy airfields and ports to check concentration of strength. They had no radar so they could not be used for shadowing at night, but the Marylands were flown with great daring and initiative and soon proved invaluable.

The following month there was a further addition to Malta's offensive power. No 48 Squadron of Wellington bombers flew into the island and began a series of raids on Mussolini's ports and shipping.

Malta had begun to hit back hard now, thanks mainly to Faith, Hope and Charity.

The remaining two Gladiators still went up against the enemy. The Hurricanes now provided the mainstay of the fighter defence, but numbers were still low and every available aircraft had to be put into the air. Throughout 1940 there were never more than six fighters in the air at one time. Four was the normal average. Enemy bombers concentrating on the airfields kept the squadron operating on a shoestring. But they went up every day and the bombers continued to operate by night.

The reconnaissance Marylands continued to do wonderful work too, and soon they were given a particularly valuable job to do.

On 28 October Italy had declared war on Greece. It now became more imperative than ever that the Italian Navy should be neutralised. Mussolini, devoted to the idea of preserving his precious 'fleet in being' sound and intact, kept his modern fast ships penned in harbour and ordered his captains to avoid contact with the British Fleet at sea. In this way he thought to keep large numbers of British warships pinned down in the Mediterranean, their strength dissipated over two thousand miles of sea. A British plan to strike at his main fleet lying smugly at anchor in Taranto harbour had been on the table for some time now, and shortly after Italy had entered the war Rear-Admiral Lyster, commanding Mediterranean Aircraft Carriers and flying his flag in *Illustrious*, had written to the C-in-C, 'They show no inclination to venture far from the Gulf of Taranto, and since it is not easy to find any inducement to make them do so, air attack in the harbour must be considered.'

If such an attack were to be made it would have to be with torpedo-bombers launched from the carriers of the Mediterranean Fleet, flown off at sea and as far as possible from the target, to avoid premature detection. This meant that the aircraft would have to make a long and hazardous flight in darkness before they arrived over Taranto. The whole operation was a delicate one, requiring detailed, meticulous preparation, and great skill on the part of the pilots and observers. It must not go off at half-cock, or it might be impossible to repeat with any promise of success.

First and foremost, the Fleet must know for certain that the enemy battle fleet was in the harbour when they made the attack, and if so, exactly where the ships were berthed. For this they relied absolutely upon good aerial reconnaissance.

The 'unsinkable aircraft carrier' anchored near Sicily did that job for them. Thanks to its small band of defenders the little 'carrier' was still 'afloat' and had been hitting the enemy itself now for some time.

The Marylands from Malta had been out over Italian ports continuously since they arrived, with Taranto the main object of their attention. The attack on Taranto was originally planned for Trafalgar Day, 21 October, but other requirements kept the fleet busy and it was postponed. Now it was to take place on 11 November – the anniversary of Armistice Day.

On 10 November aircraft from Malta were out over Taranto again. On the morning of the 11th a Fulmar arrived in Malta from the *Illustrious* to collect the latest photographs of Italian strength in the harbour. On examining these photographs Admiral Lyster and Captain Boyd of the *Illustrious* saw that five battleships and several cruisers were lying at anchor or berthed alongside – the main body of the Italian Battle Fleet. Meanwhile the Malta aircraft continued to patrol Taranto and reported later in the day that a sixth battleship had entered harbour.

The results of the epic attack at Taranto are history. When aircraft returned from their reconnaissance two days after the torpedo-bombers had done their wok their photographs showed the battleship *Littorio* laying with a heavy list and her fo'c's'le awash, one 'Cavour' class battleship with her stern under water, and one 'Duilio' class battleship beached and abandoned, while two cruisers could be seen to be heavily damaged and other ships, the seaplane base and the oil storage depot, badly knocked about.

The remainder of the Italian Battle Fleet was subsequently transferred to Naples, where it was immediately bombed by the Wellingtons from Malta, which also bombed the damaged battleship in dock at Taranto.

Taranto was a great victory and it must have been highly gratifying for the Malta fighter pilots, especially Waters, Woods, Burges and Martin, the survivors of the original few, to know that they had helped to make it possible. Without their efforts those vital sorties by the Marylands could never have been made. In that alone their struggle had its justification. They had played a vital part in keeping Malta's runways clear so that from them a gradually mounting but relentless counter-attack could take off and give blow for blow.

That the efforts of the small Royal Air Force squadron in Malta were highly appreciated is shown by the letter that the C-in-C Mediterranean wrote to Air Commander Maynard on 14 November. He said:

'My dear Maynard,
    I hasten to write you a line to thank you for the most valuable reconnaissance work carried out by

your squadrons, without which the successful attack on Taranto would have been impossible.

I well know what long monotonous flying time they have had to put in and I am very grateful to them.

The work over Taranto has been particularly valuable and gave us all we wanted to know.

Good luck and my grateful thanks again for your cooperation.

Yours very sincerely

A. B. Cunningham.'

It was nice to know that their work was thought well of. As for the fighters it was calculated that during these first five months of war, Faith, Hope and Charity and the Hurricanes had intercepted seventy-two enemy formations and destroyed or damaged thirty-seven enemy machines.

The Marylands operated under a constant threat of unserviceability. As in the case of the old Gladiators, they had no spares. They were American aircraft and their RAF maintenance mechanics could not always cater for them.

On 7 December General Wavell launched his great drive against the Italian Army in North Africa, which had advanced as far as Sidi Barrani and had there got stuck. It was vital that Wavell should be given all the air support possible, and one of the most essential needs was for accurate photographic reconnaissance of enemy bases, ports and movements. Naturally the Malta Marylands were to play a big part in this.

One day a Maryland was ordered to prepare for an urgent, top-priority mission early the next morning. Then, to the alarm of everyone it was found that the reconnaissance machines were all unserviceable – for want of tailwheel inner tubes.

Every time the Marylands landed or took off the tail wheels would 'shimmy', or otherwise castor from side to side over the rough surface of the runway. This was very hard on tyres and inner tubes, and now in fact the Marylands were out of tailwheel tubes – and there were no spares that would fit. There was only one thing to do – ring up Kalafrana.

Once again Collins found himself rushing to the airfield to see what could be done. The story of how he dealt with the problem is worth telling for the patience and skill it depicts – so typical of the way in which the men of the Repair Section did their job.

First of all Collins looked around to see what was available in the way of tubes and outer covers. He found an inner tube from a Blenheim tyre. He looked round again, trying various tyres and tubes in different combinations, but either they would not fit together or, if they did, the tube would not fit the hub of the Maryland tail wheel. And time was going on. Then, in a last frantic search, he came across an old outer cover from an enemy machine that had crashed on the island. Measuring this up with some of the other bits and pieces, he finally hit on a combination that he thought might work. The Blenheim tube he had found at first was too small for the normal Maryland outer cover, so he took the enemy outer cover and used it as a liner to fill in the space between Blenheim tube and Maryland outer cover. Then, with a bit more modification, the result was fitted to the aircraft, which subsequently took off successfully after taxying tests.

The Maryland performed its mission and returned. As it touched down on the runway at Luqa, the makeshift tyre collapsed. But it had done its job.

This was all right, but what now? He had worked a miracle for one aircraft. Now they were back where they started – he had to find some way of fixing up all the Marylands permanently.

Collins thought about it and decided to try an idea. He could get Blenheim inner tubes that would fit outer covers, but the tubes were then too big for the hubs of the wheels. He would make new hubs, or rather he would ask the dockyard to do it.

The dockyard knew him well as 'the man who never sleeps', although they were a little surprised when he walked through the gates followed by a single file of Maltese mechanics each carrying a well-filled sack over his shoulder. Collins went straight to the office of his friend Lieutenant Commander Clutterbuck, who had done many a job for him in the past. Inside, he told Clutterbuck the situation about the tyre shortage.

'Well,' said Clutterbuck, 'what are you going to do?'

'I want to have new hubs made that will take the Blenheim inner tubes,' said Collins. 'Can you do it for us?'

'Like a shot,' said Clutterbuck. 'But where's the metal corning from?'

Collins threw open the door and pointed to the three mechanics with the heavy sacks over their shoulders.

'There's the metal,' he said. He had found a number of old Swordfish propellers and had them sawn into chunks. This was what weighed the sacks down so heavily. Collins gave Clutterbuck a wooden model of the hub he wanted, the dockyard made a pattern and eventually cast the hubs that Collins required. The Marylands were soon flying again and the new hubs became standard replacement parts for the American machines.

After this Collins's reputation as an improviser increased even further. It was said that no piece of machinery or metal was safe in his vicinity, and he was always to be seen, calipers in hand, looking for some oddment that might be used to patch up an aircraft. In his duties as Aerodrome Defence Officer he worked very closely with the Army Defence Officer. It was the latter who said the last words on Collins's fanaticism. One day he had to send his runner over to Collins's office with a message. As the man turned to leave on his errand, the officer looked up from his desk.

'Oh, and don't,' he said, 'don't, whatever you do, leave your bicycle outside his office.'

The Malta machines went on with their invaluable reconnaissance flights over enemy targets.

It was from Sicilian skies, as the New Year opened, that they saw a grim sight – the Luftwaffe had arrived.

'Dearest island of all to the Sicilian is Malta, that heroic island faithfully awaiting the day of release from British slavery.'

Thus ran Goebbels's guidebook to German soldiers in Sicily. The Italians having bungled the job, they themselves were there with the express purpose of effecting that 'day of release'.

At the end of 1940 the Luftwaffe had set up an air HQ in Rome and an operational command in Sicily. In December the staff of the Nazi 10th Air Corps moved to sunny Sicily from the snows of Norway. The main strength of the unit soon followed them and the squadron messes in Sicily were full of Hitler's veterans. They brought with them 150 long-range bombers of the Heinkel 111 and Junkers 88 types, 150 Ju 87 Stukas, fifty Messerschmitt 109 fighters, and some reconnaissance aircraft. Aircraft and crews had been taken from Norway, Denmark, Holland, Belgium and France to form this force, which included some of the best and most experienced anti-shipping units in the Nazi Air Force.

Three hundred and fifty aircraft, and their target – Malta.

General Geissler, the tough and aggressive commanding officer of the 10th Air Corps, knew well of Malta's weak fighter defences. He had fifty fighters to destroy them, and three hundred bombers to reduce an island seventeen miles by nine, and he meant to show Malta the savagery of a real German blitzkrieg. He would make up for the Battle of Britain by winning the Battle of Malta.

He started on 9 January by sending some of his crack anti-shipping units against ships in Marsa Scirocco Bay. Nine Stukas, escorted by nine Italian CR 42s, made the attack. Malta read the writing on the wall and waited for the next day to bring an all-out attack.

It did not come. The German bombers were busy elsewhere.

Just after lunchtime on the 10th three low-wing monoplanes were observed approaching the island from the direction of Sicily. Some people gave them a quick look and dismissed them as Hurricanes. But one or two who knew their aircraft stared at them a little longer, saw that they were not Hurricanes, and recognised them as Fulmars, the Fleet Air Arm fighters that had been doing such good work defending the Fleet. The three Fulmars flew in over Valetta and went in to land at Hal Far. Where had they come from?

As the Fulmars were coming in to land a signal was being sent with all possible speed to all the anti-aircraft gun sites:

'Stand by – aircraft carrier *Illustrious* damaged – putting in to Grand Harbour.'

The Fulmars had come from *Illustrious*.

Somewhere away to the north-west of Malta the Axis was taking its revenge upon the ship that had hurt it so badly at Taranto. Out there in the Sicilian channel *Illustrious* was fighting for her life.

For seven hours the Stukas bombed her. After that she was a stricken ship, with two great holes torn in her armoured flight deck and a damaged rudder flinging her round in crazy circles. Her hangar deck, her wardroom and many other places between decks were a shambles of dead and wounded. As fire licked at her for'ard magazine, Captain Boyd was asked permission to flood it. He refused. Without ammunition the ship would be as good as lost. 'Better the devil you know than the devil you don't,' he thought.

With the flight deck out of action, the carrier's remaining airborne fighters, running out of fuel and ammunition, had only one course left open to them. They flew to Malta. When they took off again it was in the company of nine Hurricanes. The carrier was attempting to make the shelter of Grand Harbour and she had asked Malta for fighter protection.

An old Faith, Hope and Charity pilot led the Hurricanes. John Waters, who had by now become as skilful a pilot of Hurricanes as he had been on Gladiators, had been briefed to stand by for an immediate scramble to go and give *Illustrious* fighter cover. Then the code word for the scramble came and they were vectored towards a position north-east of Malta. They had no trouble finding the ship. When Waters approached her at a high level the ship looked like a dying stag surrounded by baying hounds. She was well down by the stern and her great, torn flight deck lay canted over at a sharp angle. Then he was diving fast into the thick of a cloud of whirling aircraft and bursting anti-aircraft shells from the 4.5s of the carrier, with which she was defending herself furiously.

'It seemed as if everything in the world was there,' he said afterwards.

There was no chance of distinguishing friend from foe and the Hurricanes and Fulmars had to take their chances as much as the Germans and Italians with *Illustrious*'s barrage. But the British pilots did their job well and shot down many of the enemy.

About six o'clock in the evening the carrier struggled slowly into Grand Harbour – bringing her convoy with her. It was a brave and deeply moving sight. The ship was listing to port and down by the stern, and it was obvious to everyone that she was finished as an aircraft carrier for many months to come. She berthed in Dockyard Creek and temporary repairs were begun so that she could sail again as soon as possible on an even keel.

The Germans watched and bided their time. Monday, Tuesday and Wednesday went by. Nothing happened – except that German reconnaissance machines came over every day, just to see how the work was getting along.

The remaining Fulmars from the *Illustrious* were now based ashore and provided a valuable addition to the island fighter defence.

All over the island people waited, worrying more than they had ever done when they had had only the Italians to face. A special box barrage was arranged to cover Grand Harbour, the carrier, and the dockyard and ships around her. When the attack came they would be protected by a great blanket of fire through which the bombers would have to pass to release their bombs on their targets.

The fighters were ready too, Hurricanes, Fulmars and two Gladiators. Once again the old biplanes were at a premium.

The Malta 'reception committee' finished its work just in time. Even as the final details were being worked out with the batteries, the Nazi squadrons were being briefed on their airfields sixty miles away to the north. Just over an hour after the last arrangements had been made in Malta, they came.

One Maltese officer was standing by at a forward observation post when the phone range. He picked it up. It was HQ.

'Can you see anything yet?' The officer raised his binoculars and strained his eyes out towards the north-west. Suddenly he stiffened and his knuckles clenched round the glasses.

Yes, they're coming. Many aircraft.'

'How many?'

After a pause he answered.

'I can count sixty aircraft crossing Grand Harbour going south.'

'Nonsense. Go and count them again.'

He did so.

'I'm sorry, I was inaccurate. I can now see sixty-five and many more in the distance.'

They came steadily, inexorably on. They went straight over Grand Harbour and on further south. Then, squadron after squadron, wave after wave, they turned, peeled off and dived – straight for the *Illustrious*.

The German pilots had courage. They went down straight through the shell-shocked air of the barrage and dropped their bombs. Straight down the path of the January sun they came as if on rails. Geysers of boiling spray leaped up from the blue waters of the harbour; a great shroud of acrid yellow smoke and choking dust arose and hung over the Three Cities immediately around the aircraft carrier as stick after stick of bombs burst across the narrow streets and yellow stone buildings. The *Illustrious* herself looked the bombers straight in the eye, her gunners ice cool, calm, and deadly accurate in the face of the roaring death so huge and black in their sights, with the guns of the *Perth* and the other ships in the harbour adding their fire to the great cloud of white-hot destruction laid by the barrage.

The first wave had been composed of Junkers 88s, which came in shallow dives from about eight or nine thousand feet, then pointed their noses at the target and let go their bombs. As the first wave retired another swarm of droning black dots appeared in the distance at ten thousand feet, coming in from the south-east, out of the sun. Again the sky over Grand Harbour blackened, then broke into screaming Stukas that hurled themselves on the crippled ship. Once again *Illustrious* completely disappeared beneath a great cloud of smoke and spray.

At first the fighters hovered outside the barrage, waiting to pounce on the enemy either just before they entered the field of danger or as they left it, wobbling and uncertain, with the machine unstable and the pilot dazed and half blacked out still from his giddy dive. In the end, however, they threw caution away and followed the Germans into the barrage.

The miracle was that the bombers hit the carriers only once, upon her quarterdeck. Their failure speaks wonders for the deadly effects of guns and fighters. 'Grand Harbour Barrage' was a hell the Nazis had not expected.

The Germans claimed next day that all their aircraft had returned safely. They overlooked the five that had fallen before the machine-guns of the fighters, the other five knocked down by the barrage, and the large number of 'probables'. One of the gunners afterwards described a victory scored by a fighter:

'I was on a light anti-aircraft gun position in the Harbour area for one of these attacks, and I can still see closely a German bomber diving through that terrific curtain of steel, followed by a Fulmar. The bomber dropped its bomb and proceeded to sneak his way out through the Harbour entrance only a few inches above the water. He was so low that he had to rise to clear the breakwater, which is only some fifteen feet high. He was obviously wobbling badly, and as he rose the Fulmar pilot shot him down into the sea on the far side of the breakwater. The Fulmar pilot then landed at his airfield, and later I received a message from him to say that he didn't think much of our barrage! However, he never flew that particular plane again, so badly was it damaged.'

They missed the *Illustrious* but they left a wasteland all around her. The Three Cities had taken most of the near misses and had suffered terribly. It was estimated that about two hundred houses had been destroyed and about five hundred more badly shattered. In Senglea the clock of the church of Our Lady of Victories had stopped at twenty past two.

The officer who had earlier reported the first wave of bombers and had been so incredulously received, saw the second attack from a different vantage point. Later he said:

'When they came the second time I was with my unit, helping to dig people out of their homes in Valetta. I had more than a hundred men digging desperately at a horrible mound of rubble, the remains of a big block of flats. All we found were three dead bodies.'

This was the real fury. Malta had had her first Nazi blitz. Now the people of Malta were one in suffering with those of Britain.

The Maltese suffered but they did not allow the blitz to interrupt their war effort. At Kalafrana the next morning a young Maltese mechanic arrived for work two hours late. When he reported to Collins, his clothes were filthy with dust, his hands cut and bleeding and black with grime. He was quite obviously dejected and weary to the point of tears.

'Very sorry I'm late, signor,' he said, 'but I have been all night searching in the ruins of my house for my wife and child.' Here he produced a crumpled photograph and burst into tears.

The three of them had been together in their home when a stick of bombs fell along the street. Telling his wife to wait, he rushed out to help as a friend's house had been demolished. While he was away another stick of bombs fell. When the dust had settled he found that his own house had been blasted into a heap of rubble. Frantically he searched the ruins, tearing the stones aside with his bare hands. All night he searched, but a new day dawned with no trace of his wife and child.

'Why have you decided to come back now?' asked Collins gently.

'Signor,' he said, 'I work on the aeroplane. I must hit back.'

Later there was a happy sequel to this tragedy. With hands dressed the lad returned to the ruins of his home and found his wife and baby safe. They had followed him out of the house and were in a nearby shelter when the house was hit. He deserved his luck.

That night the weather deteriorated and for a while the work on the *Illustrious* proceeded unmolested. But it was a fool's paradise.

On the 18th nearly a hundred aircraft bombed Hal Far and Luqa to try and destroy the fighters and make the airfields unusable before they made their final attack on the carrier. Takali had already been bogged down by the rain, and now the Germans put Luqa out of action for a time. But they did it at some cost to themselves. The fighters shot down seven of the enemy and the airfield gunners four.

Next day the attack was switched back to Grand Harbour and the *Illustrious*. Six Hurricanes, one Fulmar and one Gladiator went up. Once again wave upon wave of bombers screamed down right through the barrage, with all the fighters always close behind them.

Hurricanes, Fulmars and the lone Gladiator between them shot down eleven enemy machines that day. They seemed to have the measure of the Stukas. In addition to this the barrage claimed eight victims.

Nineteen down – a quarter of the entire attacking force, not counting probables. Said an RAF Intelligence signal: 'A good bad day with a fair score.'

There was no further blitz for a few days after this, and the repairs to the *Illustrious* were speeded up accordingly. On the 23rd she was pronounced ready for sea.

And the Gladiators very nearly went with her. Flying Officer Collins's hard-worked phone rang once more at Kalafrana. Warily he lifted the receiver. An all too familiar voice greeted him.

'Oh, Collins, Michie here. Good morning. I've got a pleasant little job for you. Dismantle the Gladiators, get them down to the dockyard, and re-erect them on board the *Illustrious*. They're wanted as fighter cover when she goes out. I think you might have to work on the flight deck if the lift is still out of action. I wish you luck. Goodbye.'

This is where I came in, thought Collins, and put a dismantling party to work at once. They took off the wings of the aircraft and made them ready for towing to the dockyard. A reconnaissance of the route was made, so that they could by-pass rubble-filled streets, and then – the phone rang again. Once again Collins put the receiver to his ear.

'Oh, Michie here,' it said. 'Wash out *Illustrious*. Her skipper says his ship will be a moving target, which is more than the island is, so our needs will be greater than his. So – get 'em flying again!'

So back they went into commission and out went the *Illustrious* without the immortal two. This time the battered carrier was unmolested. Two days after she had left Malta she arrived at Alexandria. Rome Radio announced:

'...the damage suffered is of such proportions that she will be out of service for the duration of the war.'

How they were proved wrong is another story.

The *Illustrious* had gone but the Luftwaffe had come to stay. The blitz on the carrier was only the beginning of the real siege of Malta. The German Air Force in Sicily intended to smash the Malta airfields and close her harbours to Allied ships so that they were completely useless as a base.

If they succeeded, all the Allied convoys carrying reinforcements and supplies to General Wavell would have to take the very much longer route round the Cape. If Malta was neutralised as an air base, there would be no aircraft in the central Mediterranean to interfere with General Rommel's new campaign against Wavell in North Africa.

Axis strategy depended upon Rommel smashing through to the Nile. He was their right-hand pincer. Their drive down through Greece and the Balkans was the other. Success in this two-pronged attack on the Middle East would make the Mediterranean an Axis lake. This was scheduled for summer 1941. After that, defeat of Russia by the winter would leave them free to swallow up Egypt, Palestine and Syria, and open the road to India and Persia. By the summer of 1942, Germans and Japanese would sit down together in New Delhi. That was the plan.

But first – smash Malta.

Step number one was to destroy the island's contemptible little air force. It was certainly very small, even with the reinforcements it had recently received. The Air Ministry recognised Malta's importance as an air base in February by promoting Air Commodore Maynard to Air Vice-Marshal. But they did not, could not, send him the fighters he asked for with such urgent persistence.

Meanwhile, German air strength in Sicily was increasing all the time. Fighter sweeps of Me 109s came over Malta daily and the airfields were dive-bombed savagely without pause. The island's pilots got no sleep at night and flew and fought on their nerves all day.

Day began to follow day with sickening repetition – days like the 16th, for example.

On that day two formations of Messerschmitts came over. When they saw the Hurricanes they did what they always did – split up into two groups, one dropping below and the other climbing above the Malta machines.

One Hurricane was lost that day. Later its pilot wrote in his combat report:

'Date   16.2.41

Number of enemy aircraft   10?

Type of enemy aircraft   Me 109s

Time of attack   0945 hours

Place attack was delivered   20,000ft over Luqa

No of fighter flights which took part   4 Sections of 2

Height of enemy   24,000ft

Time engagement finished   0950 hours

Height engagement finished   17,000ft

Enemy casualties   Nil

Our casualties

(a) Aircraft   One Hurricane

(b) Personnel   Left arm written off
                                                         by cannon shell.
                                                         Shrapnel in both
                                                         legs.

General report: While on patrol over Luqa at 20,000 feet, we were attacked from above and astern by six Me 109s. As previously arranged, the flight broke away to the right and formed a defensive circle. As I took my place in the circle I saw four more Me 109s coming down out of the sun. Just as they came within range I turned back towards them and they all overshot me without firing. I looked very carefully but could see no more enemy aircraft above me, so turned back to the tail of the nearest 109. I was turning well inside him and was just about to open fire when I was hit in the left arm by a cannon shell. My dashboard was completely smashed, so I bailed out and landed safely by parachute.'

The pilot was Flight Lieutenant McLachlan, a Battle of Britain veteran. John Waters and he were great friends and Waters had been leading McLachlan that day. McLachlan landed in a field, bleeding profusely. The first thing he did was to put a tourniquet on his wounded arm. Eventually he was picked up and taken to hospital. He was examined and told that they would have to take his badly wounded arm off.

'You're bloody well not!' said Mac, seeing his flying days finished.

But he had to give in, and the arm was amputated. Shortly after the operation he made a bet with his nursing sister.

'Half a crown,' he said, 'that I'll be flying again in ten days from now.' The sister humoured him and accepted the bet. Then two friends, John Waters and Tubby Elliott, came to visit him. He told them about the bet and persuaded them to help him win it.

A few days later a small car, with a rather furtive John Waters and Tubby Elliott in it, drove quietly up to the hospital and stopped at a prearranged spot. Five minutes later they were driving back to the airfield with McLachlan in the back seat. Once there, Waters and McLachlan jumped out, went across to the Station Magister aircraft and took off. When they were airborne Waters handed over the controls to McLachlan, who flew the machine a lot better with his one arm than most pilots can with two. After a short flight he handed the controls back to Waters, they landed and drove back to the hospital where McLachlan lost no time in collecting his winnings. After that, it came as no surprise later on when it was learned that McLachlan was making a great name for himself in Britain as an intruder ace – with a wooden arm in place of the one he had lost in the defence of Malta. His courage was astonishing in itself, but what was even more astounding was the fact that, whereas a man suffering from the effect of losing a limb is normally prone to severe shock if he indulges in any heavy exercise so soon after the operation, McLachlan suffered none at all – after flying an aeroplane with one hand and wounded legs.

16 February was a bad day. And there were all too many like it.

To begin with there were only a handful of aircraft to put up at all. The Fulmars and Hurricane Is were outclassed by the Me 109s and the sole remaining serviceable Gladiator took a grave chance every time it engaged the 'flying bricks' from Sicily. Outnumbered as they were, the Malta fighters never got much chance of a good attack.

You get a quick squirt at a bomber,' said one pilot, 'then the recoil of your guns pushes you out of range again and you've had it until the next time.' Again, against armoured aircraft like the Junkers 88, cannon were vital. None of Malta's machines carried them.

It was all important not to be caught napping. In order to avoid getting down-sun of enemy fighters they would patrol on the figure-of-eight principle. When there were enough machines airborne – say, eight or nine Hurricanes – and these found themselves hopelessly outnumbered, the leader would shout 'Duck duck', and the aircraft would try to form a defensive circle. By this tactic, reminiscent of fighter tactics over the Western Front in the first Great War, a pilot could cover the tail of the man in front.

The bombers came over day and night.

'There was always a Heinkel or a Junkers buzzing around, waiting to commit a nuisance,' was one pilot's recollection.

Airfields and docks, docks and airfields. So it went on, with good days and bad for the defenders, although days had become mere sophistications of the calendar. It was one long heartache, with a breather now and then.

Fighters were shot down and gun positions knocked out, but still there were Hurricanes, Fulmars and the indestructible Gladiator to take the air; still the barrage arose over Malta to catch the deadly Stukas, 88s and Heinkels in its fiery net.

Behind it all the mechanism of control functioned like a well-tended assembly line, its end product the fierce resistance of a defence that it seemed no blitz could break down.

The radar smelled out the enemy first.

'Hello Control, 40 plus A9,' went the jargon, the estimated number of attacks and a map reference.

At the Control Centre two taps were turned on, two nerve fibres quickened with the urgent message.

The RAF Controller got it, lifted his phone and said, 'Hello Hal Far. Scramble the fighters.'

And up they went, whatever machines could be flung into the air.

The Artillery Controller at his phone got it, and sent it to the officer coordinating available ships' anti-aircraft guns in the harbour and to the Gun Operations Room under St John's Cavalier. GOR sent it to the guns:

'Hostile. 40 plus. Height 10,000 feet. 360 degrees.'

At the guns they would work out a range and bearing and wait their chance, hoping for blood that day. Sometimes they were on their own. If 'No friendly aircraft airborne' or simply 'It's all yours, guns' was the word, they knew that the RAF had nothing serviceable that day. Occasionally, when the fighters were too few to be effective, they would be told to fly out south and keep out of trouble. Whatever happened, the guns opened fire when the first bandit came within range and did not stop until the last one had become a mere speck in the sky. There were recognised heights at which fighters and guns were supposed to operate, but the fighters broke the rules more often than not and came hell-for-leather down through it all to make sure of a kill. Then, and only then, a battery officer would hold his fire for a few seconds to give the fighter a chance. The porcupine withdrew its quills.

If it was a night raid, another vital arm would come alive, the searchlights. They found the victim, held him remorselessly with their unblinking eyes, and offered him, Heinkel or Junkers 88, as a fat sacrifice to guns and fighters. The island's Bofors gunners began to score heavily, their special fancy being the Heinkel 111s who came over at night to drop acoustic mines in the harbours. The Heinkels had to come down within range of the Bofors guns to lay their mines effectively. This made them easy meat. The searchlights picked them out and the Bofors knocked them down when they came low enough.

The night-fighters, too, brought the technique of cooperating with the searchlights to a fine art. But it was an art without embellishments. Crackling through the night you might hear:

'Banjo to Red One. Bandits approaching Hot Dog from north.'

'Banjo to Red One. Bandits ten miles north of Hot Dog.'

Then again: 'Banjo to Red One. Bandits five miles north of Hot Dog.'

'Banjo to Red One. Target now illuminated.'

A nerve-racking pause. Then:

'Banjo to Red One. Are you receiving me?'

No answer.

'Banjo to Red One. Are you receiving me?'

'I got the bastard.'

And at night, too, the Fleet Air Arm contrived to operate from the bumpy, crater-torn airstrips.

In February the original Swordfish squadron was reinforced by a group of Swordfish flown off the *Ark Royal* near Cape Bon.

When they arrived 'rat hunts' were still the standard procedure, as there was still no ASV equipment. They found that they would be only operating at night.

'Too bloody dangerous in daylight,' one of the veterans pointed out.

Every take-off was a nightmare, with runways like half-made roads and the ever-present German bomber droning overhead, ready to put a stop to the whole thing. Searches for likely targets usually meant a blind groping for three or four hundred miles with the promise of a hot reception when they got back to Malta from the standing patrol of Me 109s that prowled by day waiting for a striking force returning after dawn.

On 10 January the Swordfishes carried out a night-bombing raid on shipping at Palermo and kept up the good work throughout the month. On the 27th they attacked an escorted convoy, sinking two transports or supply ships for certain and leaving another badly damaged and low in the water. On the 31st they conducted a night armed reconnaissance off the Tunisian coast.

This small force was hitting the enemy, although the Luftwaffe made the number of attacks disappointing. Often the airfield would be out of action, and there were no reserves, either of aircraft or of trained aircrew to replace losses. It was Faith, Hope and Charity all over again, except that no one thought of a name for the 'rat hunters' of Hal Far. Operating at night they were unseen and unsung.

The Germans were doing well. Malta, though fighting back, was being severely checked, with every vital item for defence and attack in perilously short supply.

On 26 February thirty Ju 87s, twelve Ju 88s, escorted by twenty to thirty fighters, German and Italian, together with ten Dornier 215s and ten Heinkel 111s, attacked Luqa. Eight Hurricanes took off and the barrage round the airfield put up its fiercest display ever. At the end of the raid seven enemy bombers had been destroyed, with eleven probables. But Luqa was put out of action for forty-eight hours and six Wellingtons lay burnt out on the ground, with seven more seriously damaged.

March came in like a lion. An official signal tells the story.

'Blitz raid of several formations totalling certainly no less than one hundred aircraft, of which at least sixty bombers attacked Hal Far. A few of these aircraft dropped bombs and machine-gunned Kalafrana. Damage at Kalafrana was slight both to buildings and aircraft. One Sunderland unserviceable for few days. Damage Hal Far still being assessed.

Preliminary report as follows: Three Swordfish and one Gladiator burnt out. All other aircraft temporarily unserviceable. All barrack blocks unserviceable and one demolished. Water and power cut off. Hangars considerably damaged. Airfield temporarily unserviceable. Eleven fighters up. Enemy casualties by our fighters, two Ju 88s, two Ju 87s, one Do 215, two Me 109s, confirmed. One Ju 88 and three Ju 87s damaged. By AA, one Me 110 and eight other craft, confirmed, also four damaged. There are probably others which did not reach their base but cannot be checked. One Hurricane and one pilot lost after first shooting down one Ju 87 included above.'

This speaks plainly enough, and, between the lines, the final summary is eloquent of the situation after this deadly raid:

'For this blitz every serviceable Hurricane and every available pilot was put up and they achieved results against extremely heavy odds. The only answer to this kind of thing is obviously more fighters and these must somehow be provided if the air defence of Malta is to be maintained.'

The Swordfish attack on Rommel's tankers and supply ships in Tripoli harbour planned for that night had to be forgotten. Three of its machines lay burnt out and all the rest were out of action. This was a clear-cut round to the Germans.

Their second big achievement that day was finally to force the Wellingtons and the Sunderlands that had been operating from the island for the last few months to leave Malta for other bases out of harm's way.

General Geissler saw that his opponent was reeling. He went in for the kill, stepping up the force and fury of the daily raids and the already overpowering number of fighter sorties over Malta. The daylight patrol of 109s was increased and the Malta reconnaissance machines were hard put to operate as a result.

But he could not beat the Hurricanes. By now their numbers were low and nearly all the flight leaders had been killed. But Kalafrana continued to work miracles and the tired pilots never faltered. It was still 'Faith, Hope and Charity'. 'Strength' had not yet come to make up a quartet.

Of the Three Graces themselves, only one machine was left now. Two had been 'spitchered' on the ground, one of these in a terrible March blitz. The latter was as big a loss as a Hurricane, for in destroying it the Germans smashed a secret weapon – Squadron Leader Louks's 'Bloodiator'. In fact, Louks, who was constantly modifying his pet machine, had been meaning to take it up for a test on the very morning it was destroyed. The remaining Gladiator still went up from time to time. What the Me 109 pilots thought of her is not recorded, although it has been said by pilots who flew at the time that she made one or two of them laugh on the other side of their faces. She is even reputed to have shot one or two down, and this is not so inconceivable as it sounds when we know that on 17 March 1941 two Middle East Gladiators shot down two Me 110s without loss.

Throughout March the battered few fought on and held the Germans off from a final kill. Hurricanes and Swordfish, the only aircraft left on Malta now, were patched and put up by day and night in the face of a round-the-clock attack.

Then, towards the end of March, things began to look up once more. A convoy bringing supplies and reinforcements arrived in Grand Harbour. The Hurricanes took fresh heart and fourteen of them attacked the forty Stukas and twenty 109s that came over that day, making a dead set at the newly arrived ships. The Hurricanes shot down nine of the bombers and the guns another four, while only slight damage was done to the merchant ships in the harbour.

The Stukas had suffered severely at the hands of the Malta defenders, and it was now, when Rommel was driving hard on Egypt, that they were switched from Malta to North Africa, where the ground defences were less concentrated and it was thought that they could do more damage.

They were not missed in Malta, especially with the remainder of Geissler's bombers still keeping fighters and ack-ack defences busy. Some of the punch had gone from the attack, however, and Malta was able to breathe for a while.

The Germans now had their hands full in the eastern Mediterranean. Their great two-pronged drive against the Middle East was on. April saw the balloon go up.

Hitler invaded the Balkans, and Wavell, already hard pressed by Rommel, was forced to divide his army and send part of it to Greece. Rommel advanced steadily on Egypt.

Back in Malta, now that the full fury of blitzkrieg had temporarily subsided, the machine was beginning to run more smoothly again. At the end of March the Swordfishes began to operate once more in search of targets at sea. On 15 April a striking force that had come out from Malta in appalling weather on what turned out to be a ratless 'rat hunt', had the vicarious satisfaction of seeing Captain Mack's 14th Destroyer Flotilla, which was now working from Malta, attack and totally destroy an Axis convoy off Kerkeneh Bank. The presence of the destroyer force in Malta and this action in particular made the German bombers switch their attacks and concentrate mainly on naval targets on the island, and the battered, beaten-up airfields were able to put themselves into shape again.

Then came a minor miracle. On 2 April an RAF pilot who had fought in the Battle of Britain wrote in his diary:

'At sea. Woke to find everything vibrating like the devil, with the ship doing twenty-four knots. We have HMS *Renown* and *Sheffield* and five destroyers with us. Had a long talk from the Commander (Flying) with all the other pilots on deck-procedure for flying off. In addition to the Skuas who are leading us, we are picking up a Sunderland flying boat after about a hundred miles which will lead us the rest of the way. Had a run over my aircraft for R/T test and ran over engine. Everything OK.'

And everything remained 'OK'. They took off from the carrier at 6.20 next morning, twelve Hurricanes in two flights of six, led by two Skuas. A little while later the leading flight sighted Galatea Island. As they drew nearer they could see their Sunderland navigation escort circling round the island. The Sunderland, piloted by an ex-Imperial Airways pilot, put itself at the head of its charges and led them to Malta.

The fighters were all Hurricane Mark IIAs, a type that would be able to handle Me 109s a great deal better than the

Mark Is that were all that the defenders had had up to now.

Then, towards the end of the month, twenty-three more Hurricanes arrived. To the Malta veterans it seemed as if the sky was raining pure gold. The bombers started hitting the enemy again, and ships of the Royal Navy based on Malta took the offensive at sea.

Malta was alive *and kicking*.

CHAPTER EIGHT

Crisis

John Waters walked slowly away from dispersal towards the mess. He heard someone hailing him. It was the CO, Squadron Leader Jonas.

'John,' said the CO, as he came up, 'you're looking a bit tired. Come on over to my house. You can take your teeth out, let your hair down and we'll have a dish of rosy.'

His offer was accepted. Waters *was* a bit tired. So were they all, if it came to that, but he had had more than his share by now. He was the last of the old Faith, Hope and Charity pilots flying on Malta. Burges, Martin and Timber Woods were no longer with the squadron. Waters had been flying with the Malta fighters continuously now since the war broke out. Nearly twelve months of scrambles and bitter air battles. It was enough to be going on with, and the strain was just beginning to show.

His CO could see it. He had been watching Waters and knew that if he tried to carry on much longer he was in for trouble. It was time he was taken off flying for a while. Jonas went to the AOC at last and said: 'Sir, I want to ask you to take John Waters off flying. Otherwise he won't last much longer, he'll be shot down. He's had enough.'

A few days later Waters was posted to England. So went the last of Faith, Hope and Charity, or so it seemed.

And now yet another phase in Malta's war was about to begin.

On 27 April the Germans entered Athens. On 21 May Captain Lord Louis Mountbatten's 5th Destroyer Flotilla, which had replaced Captain Mack's 14th Flotilla at Malta, left to take part in the battle for Crete. More Hurricanes arrived for the defence of the island and Malta prepared for a renewal of the assault.

But it did not come. Hitler invaded Russia and the Luftwaffe left Sicily for the Russian front.

They had left their job unfinished. Although Malta had been partly neutralised as a naval and air base, there was still enough of both left to build on. The Hurricanes were still flying, the Swordfishes too, and submarines continued to operate from her harbours.

In London the Chief of Air Staff briefed the new AOC, RAF, Mediterranean, Air Vice-Marshal Hugh Lloyd.

'Your main task at Malta,' he said, 'is to sink Axis shipping sailing from Europe to Africa.'

Lloyd arrived in Malta in May and took over from Maynard.

The retiring AOC could look upon his achievements in Malta with pride. In the face of enormous odds his small fighter force had defended with such determination and skill that the enemy had been thrown out of his stride. Far from seeing his fighters destroyed, Maynard had seen their strength built up, in spite of heavy losses, to the two complete Hurricane squadrons now on the island, and he had initiated plans for the build-up of a greater fighter defence to come, when the island should mount a great offensive. He had built the Safi strip, between Hal Far and Luqa, to aid dispersal. In attack he had laid the foundations of Malta's future power. His development of Luqa had proved invaluable already and was to be even more so in the future. Above all he had led the Royal Air Force in Malta when it was subjected to one of the most savage maulings in its history. He had fought off the enemy and he had laid the foundation stone of victory. He had raised Malta from a military liability to a priceless asset. When he left Malta there went a great pioneer.

Lloyd set about carrying out his brief. In the lull after the Luftwaffe left, airfields and aircraft were repaired and offence operations renewed. Wellington, Swordfish and Blenheim bombers went straight to work. The Swordfishes attacked shipping with mines and torpedoes, the Blenheims beat up ships at sea from masthead height, while Hurricanes adapted as bombers strafed Sicilian airfields and the Wellingtons raided Naples and Tripoli. Malta was in business.

The fighters, too, continued their efforts. The attack on Malta had now been left to the Italians again. The Operations Book at Hal Far recorded such entries as:

'11.6.41 PM: Hurricanes intercepted enemy fighters over Hal Far. Several Macchi 200s shot down.'

The Malta fighters were now receiving regular reinforcements. A large number of Hurricanes began to come into the island, although many of these were merely on transit to the Middle East. On 2 April ten Hurricanes arrived from Gibraltar, and on the 27th fifteen more Hurricanes and two Fulmars landed. That fresh aircraft were still badly needed is shown clearly by an entry in the Operations Book.

'6.5.41 PM: Four Hurricane casualties from Hal Far as a result of enemy action.'

Three more Fulmars arrived on 9 May from the aircraft carrier *Formidable*, and on the 21st fourteen Hurricanes and four Fulmars arrived to swell the ranks. Sixteen more Hurricanes came in early June, just in time to tackle the big Italian raid on the 11th. Three days after this eleven more Hurricanes arrived from Gibraltar.

From her share of these fighters Malta soon had enough to indulge in one or two luxuries. First, night-fighting was put on a proper basis and a Malta Night Fighter Unit was officially organised to collaborate closely with the searchlights and the guns. Second, some Hurricanes were turned into light bombers. Here, ever-faithful Kalafrana was once more called upon for some clever improvisation.

By this time the stream of damaged Hurricanes had forced the Aircraft Repair Section to expand. A garage in a suburb of Valetta became a Fighter Repair Section. When the idea of turning fighters into bombers was evolved, Collins solved the problem by making bomb-rails from the Repair Section's storage racks.

Bombing was an unusual and refreshing role for the Hurricane pilots. It was a great change for them to be carrying the war to the enemy, and very satisfying for a clerkly hand to be able to record:

'9.7.41 PM: Two Hurricanes of 185 Squadron attacked sea-planes Syracuse and inflicted heavy casualties to enemy a/c.'

Another unusual job fell to the lot of the Hurricanes on 26 July. They were able to assist in a special kind of operation, after the Maltese gunners had had their share.

On the 26th Sergeant Zammit of the Royal Malta Artillery was on duty with his gun at Fort St Elmo.

'Suddenly, I heard the sound of an MTB and although it was still twilight I saw a small MTB three hundred yards away heading towards the breakwater bridge. I gave the alarm and my gun went into action just as the MTB hit the bridge and blew up. Searchlights illuminated the scene. A hundred yards away from the bridge I saw another small craft. I directed the gun on to it and with the first two shots hit it and blew it up. I again directed the gun on to a third one a hundred yards away and with the first few rounds it was destroyed. I saw three others heading towards Grand Harbour. All guns fired at them. One was destroyed and two disabled. About a quarter of an hour later I saw too small suspicious objects at about 2,000 yards away. I directed the gun on to one of them. After ten to fifteen seconds they moved and I opened fire immediately. A couple of seconds later all other guns engaged.

At this moment I saw them zig-zagging, manoeuvring and cleverly turning about at a high speed to avoid the very heavy punishment. They were sunk.

The scene of red and green tracers bouncing sky high from the sea, and the noise of the guns together with the shouting and applause of the civilians on the roof tops and bastions was like a firework display on a festive occasion.

Just after all this I saw two large MTBs far away and out of range of my gun. These were being engaged by the Hurricanes.'

So failed Malta's only seaborne attack. The Hurricanes pursued the retreating enemy and sank four, damaging several others. The Italian attacking force, a mixed one of E-boats and 'human torpedoes', was routed and almost annihilated.

The Maltese took this victory as a sign that their island had really begun to hit back, as indeed it had. For example:

'Offensive. Night, 16th-17th October. Sixteen Wellingtons bombed Naples. Total bombs dropped: 36,000lbs, including three 4,000 pounders and sixteen 1,000 pounders.

Day 17th October: six Blenheims with Hurricane escort bombed seaplane base Syracuse.'

Malta submarines, too, were out sinking enemy ships, and more reinforcements of Hurricanes were flown in from carriers. A young pilot writing in his diary gives us an idea of what such an operation was like:

'Wed 13 Nov 1941:

Our first flight took off the *Argus* when the Blenheims turned up at 10.15am. All took off OK except Pilot Officer L–. He had never flown a long-range Hurricane before. He swung violently to port. He nearly killed me and several others. His wing passed over W–, H–, B– and me as he went off over the side a little higher up the deck. I just had time to think: "Thank goodness I've got fat J H– in front of me." Then I looked forward and down expecting to see L– in the sea, but he wasn't, he was flying and his wheels were retracting too. Very lucky, for he'd broken the flag flying from the *Argus*, and had almost knocked off his tail wheel, which came off when he landed at Malta.

An hour later we took off with two more Blenheims which arrived from Gib; but not before I'd been choked by the fumes, for my machine, BG 713, was over the funnel. The apparent wind speed over the deck was 35-40 knots, so, though I had only 400-450ft, I found the take-off easy enough.

The Blenheims really navigated very well. The visibility was bad yet they found our ships at point X (off Algiers) and took us to Malta, only sighting land, the African coast, two or three times, with no horizon and only seeing the sun once or twice. I think it was near Cape Bon that we went down to sea level and flew for some two hundred or more miles at nought feet to avoid being fixed by the Italian radio locators. I thought I heard someone call on the R/T very faintly when we were off the neighbourhood of Cape Bon, but it was not one of my flight and there was nothing I could do – we had to keep R/T silence except in extreme emergency.

About 2.45 or 3 o'clock we came at last out of bad visibility over Gozo. Landed at Hal Far, in Malta. Sergeant W– has landed somewhere else on the island – goodness knows why – landed at 3 or 3.15 o'clock. One of 242 Squadron landed wheels up in front of me. (He'd been unable to get them down.) I think I had 30 or so gallons of fuel left, though some of the others saw they had as many as 70 gallons over.

Two sergeant pilots are missing – Sergeant – 242, and Sergeant –, also 242 Squadron. One turned off for North Africa and the other, after an hour, turned back to try and find the ships. Whether they will ever be heard of again is unlikely.

This island is odd. It protrudes abruptly out off the sea: yet no point on the island rises to any great height. It is like a uniformly even piece of rock at a distance from the air.'

With the British Eighth Army beginning its advance into Cyrenaica, things were starting to look black for Rommel.

In fact, so seriously did Hitler view the situation that he withdrew squadrons from the Russian front, where they were badly needed, and sent them to Sicily.

From January until May Malta suffered a blitz of unparalleled savagery. This time the Germans were determined to destroy all opposition on Malta, regardless of the cost to themselves.

They nearly succeeded. Beginning with an average of fifty to seventy-five sorties a day and increasing the number to over three hundred on peak days, a massed air blitz smashed Malta relentlessly, working right round the clock.

Bit by bit, inexorably, they reduced the historic loveliness of Valetta to ruins, smashed the harbours and eased the pressure on Rommel's convoys supplying his big push on Egypt. The Axis radio announced ad nauseam the subjugation of the island. Malta, the 'unsinkable aircraft carrier', soon vied with the *Ark Royal* in the number of times she had been 'sunk'. The Axis announcer was a little premature when he said:

> 'We know that we have broken the spell of Malta and that our effort has brought out a decision in the Mediterranean struggle.'

Somehow the struggle still seemed to be going in, however – 'At least, that was my impression,' said a naval pilot at Hal Far.

The island's striking forces, hamstrung by bombing and by a period of appalling weather, when torrential rains made Hal Far and Takali unusable for days on end and Luqa consequently very overcrowded, continued to operate, and even at the height of the blitz early in March, Wellingtons dropped 26 tons of bombs on an Axis convoy in Palermo harbour. But soon the weight of the Malta attacks dwindled under the continual pounding. The few Hurricanes left fought desperately on, the small force reduced once more to Faith,

Hope and Charity proportions. Then, at long last, their prayers were answered.

An Australian pilot, one of those who had taken off from a carrier that morning on the last leg of their journey to Malta, saw his new base first as a tiny speck against the horizon. The little island seemed to him to be floating just above the surface of the sea like a cloud. They flew straight in along the path of the sun towards it. Ten miles out he heard Control.

'Hello, Exile boys. Keep on your present course. Watch out for 109s below.'

He didn't like the sound of that. They dropped down low on the water as they approached the island. To the north, uncomfortably close, he could see Sicily – just a flat, thin line of beach with a line of cumulus above it, and, beyond it, Etna, with her top covered in snow. Sicily meant trouble. That was where the 109s came from. He knew that the Germans kept a big standing patrol of Schmitts over Malta. *OK, let 'em come, I'm tired of sitting up here watching the bloody clock, getting pins and needles in my arse.* But they didn't see any Schmitts that day.

As they came in he had a good look at the island that he had heard likened to an unsinkable aircraft carrier. She did look a bit like a ship at that, a great ship with her sheer sides disappearing into deep water. As he looked down he saw brown cliffs and below them pale green shallows with a line of foam as white as coconut meat. Right in the 'middle of the island a big round church dome stood out. He saw the great, battered pile of white and yellow buildings around Grand Harbour and a patchwork of little bright fields all round. Then the leader picked out Takali and they came in to land. At the last minute he couldn't get his undercarriage down and had to use the emergency gear. When he did get down he looked around him. Takali seemed very small and rough, and all the buildings were in ruins. The airfield was deeply scarred all over and the dispersal he walked to was just a heap of rubble. What the hell are we in for, he thought.

To Malta their arrival was like a breath of spring, for they brought the first Spitfires. There were only fifteen of them, but they were all priceless. The new boys soon learned the Malta story.

'Well, chaps,' said an old veteran of twenty-two, 'you'll find Malta a bit different from the UK. None of those lovely big fighter sweeps here. No more tea in bed.'

'No,' said a Canadian voice, 'Jerry does all the fighter sweeps here.'

'Yeah – fifty plus at a time,' chipped in a Springbok. A Scottish pilot took up the dirge.

'I'll give you a tip,' he said soberly, 'out of the kindness of my heart. In fact it's a golden rule out here. *Always keep your tail clean*. When you've got a nice fat 109 in just the right position – that's the time to look behind you, because there's probably five or six of his pals on your tail with their fingers all set to give you a squirt.'

The briefing they received was clear-cut.

'The Spits will operate four or eight at a time,' they were told. 'They will cover the Hurries on their climb up, engaging and keeping the 109s busy while the Hurries deal with the bombers.'

On 10 March, three days after they had arrived, the new Spitfires put this plan into action. In that first encounter they shot down one 109, probably destroyed two, and badly damaged one more. Then a spell of exceptionally bad weather kept both sides grounded and gave Malta a short breather.

Then it began all over again and Malta was soon fighting for her life. A March convoy was cruelly savaged and only part of it reached Malta. The Luftwaffe then staged an all-out attack on the few ships unloading at the quays and on all shipping and dock installations.

The Spitfires were up to their necks in the fighting. Their plan of battle soon went adrift. There were so many 109s that the Malta fighters were practically swamped. It was a free-for-all every time with everyone taking on three or four Messerschmitts. They destroyed many enemy planes, bombers as well as fighters, and sustained heavy losses themselves until, once more, the small fighter force was reduced to a handful.

In April a second squadron was re-equipped with Spitfires, but many aircraft were destroyed on the ground and once again the Hurricanes took the main defence upon their strong backs. Sometimes ten or a dozen Hurricanes engaged a hundred or more German aircraft. More often there would only be four Malta fighters in the air with another two in reserve for airfield defence. In this case the Faith, Hope and Charity technique was invariably used. The four attacking Hurricanes would scramble at the first sign of the enemy and climb as fast as they could into the sun. To save aviation spirit, which was by now in desperately short supply, the last two aircraft were held until the last possible minute, then sent up to do what they could against the hordes of enemy aircraft that, after the blitz against the March convoy, made a dead set once more at the airfields. In strict radio silence the Hurricanes would fly out to a point twenty or thirty miles to the south of the island until Control switched them to whichever airfield was in direst need of their services. They usually arrived to find the battered few of the British attacking force, their ammunition gone, being heavily attacked by Messerschmitts flying insolently in the airfield circuit.

By now the Germans were flinging three or four hundred sorties a day at Malta. Half of these would be bombers unloading about 350 tons of bombs daily between them. The targets were the airfields and docks, though sometimes it was simply anything that stood upright – churches, hospitals, schools, even farmers in their fields and children playing in the open. In the rock shelters Maltese women prayed:

'*Qalb ta' Gesu ta' Marija itfghu il – bombi fil –*
bahar jew fil – hamrija!
(Sacred heart of Jesus and of Mary, make the bombs go in the sea or in the soil!)

One old woman begged continually. 'O Lord, send over the Italians!'

And now Malta was being starved out. Cut off from the rest of the world, her food and fuel supplies got so low that a 'starvation date' was set for mid-August. But they fought on.

Now, as in the great siege four hundred years before, the eyes of the civilised world were upon Malta. Then, the reigning British sovereign, Elizabeth I, had said:

'If the Turks should prevail against the Isle of Malta it is uncertain what further peril might follow to the rest of Christendom.'

Not the Turks now, but a greater, viler scourge had fastened itself upon decent humanity everywhere. Now Christendom was in even greater peril.

And now another great British monarch took the name of Malta. On 15 April 1942 His Majesty King George VI sent this message to the people of the wonderful little island:

'To honour her brave people I award the George Cross to the island fortress of Malta to bear witness to a heroism and devotion that will long be famous in history.'

The King and his ministers, the men of the fighting services, had long known of Malta's fight. Now the whole world would know the glorious things that were happening there.

The defenders fought on with new heart. Three days after the King's announcement, a large reinforcement of Spitfires was flown in from the American carrier *Wasp*. But Malta still had much to suffer. Three days after they had landed all the new Spitfires were unserviceable. The Germans had made them their special target and had shattered them on the ground, many of them while their motors were still running from their first landing in Malta.

At the end of April things were desperate. Two hundred enemy machines had been shot down during the month by fighters and guns, but in the bitter air battles that had raged twenty-three Spitfires and eighteen Hurricanes had been lost, while eighty-seven more fighters lay badly damaged and out of action. The guns were being rationed for ammunition now, and the gallant 10th Submarine Flotilla, which had continued to operate from the island throughout the very worst of the previous attacks, was at last forced to leave.

Though full of fight still, Malta now had no sword to strike with and little strength left with which to shield herself from the increasingly savage blows of the enemy. On 27 April the AOC signalled that enemy operations might soon prove disastrous unless immediate steps were taken to counter them. He could not tolerate, he said, the enemy's ability to operate unmolested.

Then, just after this signal had been sent out, the noise of battle died down. It did not cease entirely, and in fact Malta was under attack for several more months, but when one afternoon the sirens sounded and no Germans appeared it seemed as if someone had put back the clock. To help this impression the Italians appeared, flying in tight formation at a great height, just as they had on that first day of war when Timber Woods had shot down the first enemy over Malta. On 29 April there had been 220 sorties against the island. The next day there were only sixty-eight.

The Luftwaffe had failed. All these months, with the army in Russia crying out for more air support, the defenders of Malta had tied down several hundred first-line German aircraft in the Mediterranean. These aircraft had certainly helped Rommel to go forward in the desert by reducing the Malta striking force, but in doing so they had taken too long about it. In their ultimate objective they had failed utterly. They left Malta with their real job undone, with the island still intact and in Allied hands. Many of their units had to be withdrawn to other fronts and the remainder rested and repaired.

Malta took full advantage of the lull. May came in with the promise of better things to come. In particular the defenders now looked forward to the promise of sixty-four new Spitfires due to arrive on the 9th. Three days after this HMS *Welshman* was expected with supplies and ammunition. The tired and starving island waited, living on hope.

This time nothing must go wrong. News of the promised Spitfires had only come through on the 7th, so there were only days in which to work out a comprehensive plan to ensure their safe arrival and that of the *Welshman* later.

To this end the airfields were given top priority for anti-aircraft defence during the landing of the Spitfires. All ammunition and target restrictions were to be lifted after dawn on 8 May, and the system of rest and relief at the guns was cancelled for the time being. On the arrival of the Spitfires heavy barrages would be put up over the airfields while the machines would come in very low to give the gunners a chance.

On the morning of Saturday 9 May they started coming in. At first many people dashed instinctively for cover, because, as one of the pilots put it, 'On Hal Far as soon as you heard anything you dived for shelter. You didn't stop to ask what made the noise.' Then they looked up again and saw the tapering wings of Spitfires sharp across the sky – scores of them.

The Germans saw them too, and came over at their leisure for the usual bore of bombing Spitfires on the ground. But the cupboard was bare. Then the Spitfires that they had expected to find squatting on the airfields fell upon them out of the sun. Within thirty minutes of the first Spitfire touching down on Malta, the entire new force was airborne again, refuelled, rearmed and waiting for the Germans. In some cases a Spitfire landed and took off again inside five minutes, so smoothly had the new arrangements worked.

As soon as a Spitfire landed it was met by a soldier or airman who directed it to a dispersal pen. Here, petrol, oil, glycol and ammunition were immediately fed into the machine, while the new pilot scrambled out of the cockpit and, as far as possible, was replaced by an experienced Malta pilot, who took off the instant the aircraft was ready. Maintenance men, pilots and relief pilots lived all day at the pens, all of which were in communication with each other by wireless, despatch rider or signalman. In this colossal task the Army gave priceless help, supplying men and equipment.

All day the air battle raged. 'Ate lunch in the aircraft,' said one new Malta pilot in his diary, 'as I was at the ready till dusk. After lunch we were heavily bombed again by eight Ju 88s.' He goes on, 'Scrambled again in the same section after tea – no luck again. One Spit was shot down coming in to land and another at the edge of the airfield. Score for the day, seven confirmed, seven probables and fourteen damaged for the loss of three Spits.'

There were nine raids that day. The fighters shot down seven of the enemy with many probables and the guns destroyed one aircraft and two probables. Next morning the *Welshman* entered Grand Harbour. A few minutes after she had berthed the alert sounded and the Germans were on her.

They were in for several shocks. First they found that they had to make their approach to the target through a dense smoke screen and an intense barrage, which grew denser and fiercer as the special naval and RAF working parties unloaded more and more ammunition and smoke containers from the cruiser. And there were Spitfires everywhere.

Some of the new boys had a busy day. One of them wrote:

'We climbed up to 4,000 feet, and then the barrage was put up by the harbour defences and the cruiser. The CO dived down into it and I followed close on him. We flew three times to and fro in the barrage, trusting to luck to avoid the flak. Then I spotted a Ju 87 climbing out at the fringe of the barrage and I turned and chased him. I gave him a one-second burst of cannon and he broke off sharply to the left. At that moment another Ju 87 came up in front of my nose and I turned into him and let him have it. His engines started to pour out black smoke and he started weaving. I kept the tit pushed hard, and after a further two-to-three-second burst with the one cannon I had left, the other having jammed, he keeled over at 1,500 feet and went into the drink.

I then spotted a 109 firing at me from behind and pulled the kite round to port, and after one and a half turns got on his tail. Before I could fire another 109 cut across my bows from the port side and I turned straight on his tail and fired till my cannon stopped through lack of ammo. He was hit and his engines poured out black smoke, but I had to beat it as I was now defenceless and two more 109s were attacking me.'

Fifteen enemy aircraft were destroyed that day by the fighters and eight by the guns, with many seriously damaged probables. Three Spitfires were shot down, with the loss of only one pilot. The *Welshman* was completely unloaded in five hours.

This was a pronounced victory. At last, at long last, the thrill of success went round the island.

And after this Malta never really looked back. Germans and Italians kept up their attacks, especially at night, but made such little headway against the garrison, which was heavily forced by Spitfires and Beaufighters, that their first fury began to diminish. Malta's bomber offensive soon began to mount again, against shipping at sea, and the enemy's ports and bases.

It was only to be expected that the Germans would try again to destroy that thorn in their flesh, which now threatened to become sharper than ever. As July began they increased the pressure again. Once again the defenders found themselves under siege. This time, however, they had more weapons to fight back with. A Canadian pilot who came to Malta at this time with a new Spitfire squadron says:

'We flew in on 7 June. It was like waking from a sweet dream into the heart of an earthquake. Scared? You never got time to be scared on Malta. What a show! Bombs whistling round your ears, Spits and Me's weaving all over the sky, and every once in a while some poor devil who hadn't kept his tail clean spinning down in flames. Flak went up in flowerbeds and parachutes came drifting down. From the ground the roar of ack-ack batteries going twelve hours a day

'– up high the clatter of machine-gun and cannon bursts and the roar of full-engined Spitfires, Me's and Macchis diving... Men scurrying about the drome patching bomb craters... Engineers detonating time bombs... Rescue launches rushing to sea to pick up floating parachutists... The Maltese trying to carry on the day's chores between headlong dives for the shelter... Cats and dogs fighting in the streets in keeping with the tempo of the place. Never a dull moment day or night.'

On 14 July Air Vice-Marshal Lloyd relinquished his command, having been an inspiration to all throughout this dark time. He was succeeded by Air Vice-Marshal Sir Keith Park, who had commanded a fighter group in the Battle of Britain. In a Special Order of the Day the new AOC was able to announce:

'Our day-fighter strength has during June and July been greatly increased and the enemy's superiority in numbers had long since dwindled. The time has now arrived for our Spitfire squadrons to put an end to the bombing of our airfields by daylight. We have the best fighter aircraft in the world, and our Spitfire pilots will again show their comrades on the ground that they are the best fighter pilots in the world.'

Park introduced a 'forward interception plan' whereby his fighters, aided by improved radar, intercepted the enemy formations before they reached the coast of Malta. By this method German and Italian fighters and bombers were shot down into the sea in large numbers, while the Malta airfields were able to get on with the job of putting a heavier and heavier striking force into the air.

But the island was still under siege, and all essential commodities, including petrol, were heavily rationed. On 20 June the AOC had been compelled to signal to the Chief of Air Staff:

'Until further supplies of 100 octane reach this island all available 100 octane must be used for defence.'

In August the remains of the battered 'Ohio' convoy came into Grand Harbour and there was some relief for the besieged. The AOC was able to signal that, provided air superiority could be maintained, ten weeks' fuel could now be added to the four weeks' stock that was all that had remained in hand before the convoy arrived.

In spite of the need to conserve fuel, however, Malta's offensive grew. Its main target now was Rommel's line of supply from Europe. All through the summer bombers from Malta attacked his convoys going from Italy to Africa. Bombs and torpedoes smashed supply ships and tankers and made the seas around the island so dangerous for Axis shipping that ships had to be re-routed by long and uneconomical tracks to reach North African ports. The short, convenient route from Naples through the Straits of Messina to Benghazi, and that between Malta and the coast of Tunisia to Tripoli, had to be virtually abandoned. Instead, more distant routes via the east, hugging the Greek coast, had to be used, at a time when British and German armies were facing each other at El Alamein, each struggling to build up their resources to dominant strength.

On 11 October, with the battle of El Alamein about to open, the Luftwaffe staged one final, all-out blitz upon Malta, 'to keep,' as Berlin Radio announced, 'the British squadrons grounded and to deny access to the port of Valetta.'

Far from being 'grounded', the Malta squadrons met the Germans half way from Sicily and utterly routed them. In all, the Germans threw six hundred aircraft against Malta. Fighters and guns destroyed 204 of them, for a loss of thirty-one machines.

No airfield on the island was out of action during this time for more than thirty minutes, and there was only one night when the Malta bombers did not go out against shipping. For the enemy this was utter failure. On 23 October the Eighth Army attacked and soon began to drive Rommel back along the coast.

In November, after Malta aircraft had taken a big part in the North Africa landings and had begun heavy raids on Sicily, a big convoy arrived, unharmed, in Grand Harbour, with bands playing and wave upon wave of cheering rising from the people lining the walls of Valetta.

The siege was raised. Now Malta was entirely free to give her thoughts, her energy and resources and all the strength made fiercer by ordeal, to the one task of attacking and destroying the enemy.

Malta soon grew fat with whole wings of Spitfires. There was no sign of an old biplane fighter with a fixed undercarriage.

The last Gladiator had been a victim of the siege. For some time she had remained in use as a meteorological aircraft. Pilots would take the old machine up with various instruments attached to its struts, then, suddenly aware that they had a thoroughbred under them, forget the dull job they had come up to do and indulge in a display of aerobatics, which the old aircraft would perform without flinching, quite putting Spitfires and Hurricanes and Beaufighters to shame. Many a dog-fight ended with the Gladiator on the tail of a Spitfire.

'Climb like a dingbat,' said the pilots who had come to scoff. 'Absolute pure gold.'

She escaped the vicious bombing for some time, but her luck could not last.

The Gladiator, says an official report, 'was ... housed in a pen at Hal Far which was bombed with disastrous results to the aircraft. It was recovered from the wreckage of the pen, the engine and wings removed for salvage, and the fuselage parked in a disused quarry pending collection. Owing to more urgent commitments it was forgotten...'

It was quite natural. There *were* 'more urgent commitments'. So, while Albacores, Beauforts, Wellingtons and Blenheims went out on their victorious raids, while Spitfires and Beaufighters in scores shot the Luftwaffe out of the Mediterranean sky, the sole survivor of the island's first defenders, the brave three who had made this great offensive possible, lay rotting in a quarry.

CHAPTER NINE

Faith

It was over – the struggle, the weariness, the sweat. Malta had won. She had broken out of her circle of besiegers and her aircraft and ships were hunting them down. Airmen, soldiers, sailors and civilians alike, they had saved her from her enemies.

One day, into the Aircraft Repair Section at Kalafrana came a load of old aircraft components for salvage. There, among the collection of junk, someone noticed an old, bent and battered fuselage. This relic turned out to be the wreck of an old Gladiator.

It was one of the weapons that, in the hands of those brave few, had saved Malta from the Italians in that distant, desperate time of the island's first peril. This broken and mutilated survivor and its three companions had saved, so many people said, the whole delicate balance of power in the Mediterranean. This wreck had been the weapon of victory.

Yes, to this old bag of bones the new crusaders owed it all, to this and three other old warriors, long-destroyed, and to the men who had flown them in those far-off days. If they had failed, those few, there would have been no offensive, no enemy convoys sunk, no ports and bases pounded, and, perhaps, no victory. For if there had been no fighters in the air on that vital day in 1940, what might the arrogant Regia Aeronautica have done to an undefended island, emboldened further by an almost completely clear field?

As it was, their overwhelming confidence suffered a shock from which it never recovered. And the defenders themselves took greater courage from the example set them.

If they had not been there... It is not difficult to imagine Mussolini in Valetta, after all, and Axis aircraft and ships using Malta as the Allies used it later. The possible effects of such a calamity upon the Allied situation in the

Mediterranean and ultimately on the course of the whole war are very plain.

But they *were* there, and in the end there was a victory.

So it occurred to some that it would be a fine thing to preserve this battered weapon and display it for ever in a place of honour along with the bright armour of the Knights of St John and the great sword of La Valette.

The old nickname was recalled of 'Faith, Hope and Charity'. By consulting records and the memories of those who had served on the Maltese airfields when the three Gladiators had operated, it was concluded that the surviving aircraft was the one generally known as 'Faith'. Something must be done, they said, before the old fuselage on its undercarriage stumps and tyreless wheels was broken up for scrap.

Something was done. Late on a bright afternoon in September 1943 the aircraft 'Faith' was publicly presented by the Royal Air Force to the people of Malta.

The presentation was made at six o'clock on Friday 3 September 1943, by the AOC Royal Air Force, Malta, Air Vice-Marshal Sir Keith Park, to his Honour the Chief Justice of Malta, Sir George Borg.

The guard of honour drawn up round the dusty square was called to attention as the AOC appeared in the Palace entrance. As he took his place at the dais the guard commander gave the salute, 'Guard of Honour, Air Salute, Present Arms', his voice echoing round the square. The band of the Royal Malta Artillery then played the Air Salute and the AOC made an inspection of the guard.

Out in the middle of the square, with the upright guards saluting her, was the object of the ceremony. 'Faith' stood upright, her frame polished now and painted a bright silver, the fine bones of her skeleton gleaming in the hard sunlight. The sky above her yawned empty and blue where she had once flown and fought. She stood at rest, stripped and exposed, as if to say, 'This is all there was between you and the murderous anger of your enemies, this frail machine that once turned and dived and glided in the sunlight at twenty thousand feet like a silver fish in its crystal element.' Then the two representatives of the peoples who had fought so closely together in the great siege of Malta paid their separate tributes to the honoured veteran that stood before them. Sir Keith Park spoke first.

'Before presenting this famous old Gladiator to the people of Malta, I shall give you a brief account of the part she played in the defence of this island.'

From there the AOC went on to tell the main outline of the story that has been told in these pages. In conclusion he said:

'From these small beginnings was built the fighter defence of Malta, which in July 1942 put a stop to the daylight bomber raids by intercepting the enemy and smashing up his formations before they could reach Malta. In this month of July, our Spitfires destroyed 137 enemy aircraft for a loss of only eighteen fighter pilots.

In October 1942, less than a year ago, the Axis attempted their final daylight blitz on Malta. Greatly superior numbers of bombers and fighters, the largest there had ever been concentrated in Sicily, launched the final blitz, but, again, the Spitfires smashed the enemy bomber formations away north of Malta before they could reach their target. In ten days our Spitfire squadrons destroyed 118 aircraft for a loss of thirteen fighter pilots.

The defence of Malta can justifiably be included among the epics of this war, and "Faith" has earned a place of honour in the armoury of Malta. The part played by "Faith", "Hope" and "Charity" is symbolic of the courage and endurance displayed by the people of Malta during the long struggle against vastly superior Axis Air Forces.

It gives me great pleasure now to hand over this famous old fighter, "Faith", to his Honour Sir George Borg, as a gift to the people of Malta.'

The Chief Justice then acknowledged the gift on behalf of the people of Malta. He said:

'In my darkest days of the great siege, which, thanks to the Governor's wise guidance, with the help of the three fighting forces, the enemy has now been compelled to abandon, three rays which popular imagination styled "Faith, Hope and Charity" radiated from the unsinkable aircraft carrier, placed by nature in the heart of the blue Mediterranean sea, to defy the swarms of locusts which mercilessly devastated this bulwark of the Empire and threatened to break the great link uniting its remotest outposts to the Mother Country.

And well they did perform their task, guided by hearts of oak who defied the immensely superior power of a ruthless enemy. And well they did symbolise the unswerving Faith which the people of Malta always had in the invincible nation that protects them, the never-failing Hope of ultimate victory, then apparently so remote, the smiling rays of Charity that would mete out mercy to the vanquished but ask for none. And these islands that withstood three thousand air raids witnessed the phenomenal increase of air power from a tiny nucleus into thousands of wings which attacked the whole African coast, hindering the enemy's supplies to his armies that had threatened the land of the Pharaohs. As General Eisenhower very pertinently stated recently, the forces based on Malta played no little part in the conquest of Sicily. No more tangible proof could be afforded of the immense resources of the Allied Nations, and no better warning could indeed by given to those sinister powers that dared wake the Lion from its slumber.

It is therefore with a sense of pride, not unmingled with gratitude, that I today, Sir Keith Park, receive from you on behalf of my fellow countrymen one of those three aeroplanes to be jealously safeguarded as an everlasting remembrance of the ordeal the men under your command together with the people of Malta have passed in the hour of the great trial. This aeroplane will always remind us of the gratitude my countrymen owe to the Royal Air Force, of which you are so distinguished a representative. I hope I may be allowed publicly to express Malta's thanks for the several marks of favour which have been shown to this tiny outpost of the Empire; the high honour His Majesty the King was pleased to confer on the Maltese, by presenting them with the George Cross; the promise of self-government; the grants in aid; the unexpected visit which His Majesty paid to his faithful Maltese subjects; and last but not least the presentation of this symbol of unity, faith and charity, which you, Sir Keith Park, are today making, will all contribute to cement the proverbial loyalty of the Maltese people towards the Crown that protects them.

I feel sure to be interpreting the unanimous view of my countrymen in assuring you, and through you all the members of the fighting forces, of our deep admiration for the courage, fortitude and resolution they are constantly displaying on land, on the sea and in the air. Like the Maltese people, they are suffering and fighting for a common cause, for a great ideal which is dearest to the human heart, the ideal to live freely and to enjoy the blessings of our great Christian civilisation.'

And so this creature of the singing altitudes, of the high, wide, sunny spaces of the free air, this trusty old friend, was given a state funeral and put away in a museum. She rests there now, in the armoury of the Palace of the Grand Masters in Valetta.

During the later war the contents of the armoury, like so many other fine works of art, went underground. Old paintings, swords, tapestries and exquisitely wrought suits of armour were stored down in the rocky bowels of the island out of harm's way. There they suffered considerably from damp and bad storage, so badly in fact that it took nearly five years to clean them all and restore them to their previous state of repair.

But they are all to be seen now in their beauty and richness. There are solid, highly wrought and polished brass cannon from the eighteenth century, pikes, swords, guns and pieces of shining steel armour. There is the heavy 'sapping armour' of Aloph de Wignacourt, shield, breastplate and chapel-de-fer, and the half-length suit of armour of subtle Milanese art worn by Grand Master La Valette at the first great siege. There too is the glittering full-length panoply of Martin Garzes, the masterpiece Sigismund Wolf of Landshut made for the Grand Master, and the full armour wrought by Geronimo Spacini of Milan for de Wignacourt, in which he was painted by Lionello Spada.

And at the end of the armoury, facing these treasures, is the aeroplane 'Faith'. She stands there on the metal rims of her wheels, with her old, two-bladed wooden propeller still, and two of her black machine-guns at her sides. If you duck underneath her battered fuselage you can see the deck-landing hook still in place in its triangular bed. If you are lucky you may perhaps be able to persuade the guide to let you climb up on the stump of a wing and swing your leg over to sit and look out over the high nose at the big black airscrew.

Tourists come to the armoury and have their photographs taken in surprised and slightly shamefaced groups round the old aircraft. Modern jet pilots from Hal Far come and examine her critically, wondering what she was like to fly. For she is a relic now, and will never fly again, only stand here among the pikes and brass cannon and cunningly wrought armour, collecting dust, yawned at by visitors and school parties. The plaque on the table underneath her nose reads:

'*Gloster Gladiator Aircraft N.5520*

This is "Faith" the sole survivor of the three Gloster Gladiator Aircraft, known as FAITH, HOPE and CHARITY which fought alone against the Italian "Regia Aeronautica" between June and October 1940. She survived all her combats and was replaced by Hurricanes finally to be put out of commission by an enemy bomb in a hangar at Hal Far Air Station.

Presented to the people of Malta by Air Vice-Marshal Sir Keith Park KBE CB MC DFC on behalf of the Royal Air Force on September 3rd 1943.'

If you should ever go into the armoury of the Grand Masters and see the old aircraft, go and look at the name, FAITH, inscribed just below the cockpit on her starboard side. Look at the name and remember what it stands for.

Remember the men who gave their lives to keep her in the air, the men who toiled to keep the runway fit for her to fly from. Above all, remember the men who flew her and the debt we all owe to them. Remember too the men who followed these pioneers, men from England, Ireland, Scotland and Wales, from Canada, Australia, New Zealand, South Africa and the United States, who fought for freedom in the skies above Malta.

'Faith' is the symbol of their courage and their will to win. It is the password of the breed that produced them.

Postscript
to the original 1954 edition

In April 1952 Wing Commander George Burges gave a broadcast on the subject of the early air defence of Malta in which he played so notable a part. In the course of the broadcast he paid tribute to all 'the other members of the team' who, in company with his own Service, helped to save Malta:

'Above all to the Royal Navy and to the Merchant Service who at great cost to themselves brought convoys through to Malta from both the East and the West. This was our lifeline, without which neither the defence nor the offensive operations could have been sustained.

Nor was that all the Royal Navy did for us. When aircraft could not be flown for want of some vital spare part which was not available in the island, the resourceful Dockyard made it for us from whatever raw material happened to be handy. For instance – when we ran out of spare tailwheels for Maryland reconnaissance aircraft the Dockyard made us some out of old airscrew blades.

We also had good reason to be grateful to the Army – although they did shoot at us once or twice in their enthusiasm instead of the enemy. In addition to their own job they not only repaired our airfields after enemy attacks but also helped in servicing the fighters as well.

I would like also to say how much we appreciated the support received from the people of Malta and hope that to some extent we justified their confidence in us. The tasks of the Civil Administration must have been difficult in the extreme, but the various Government departments were always ready to give us such assistance as was within their power.

My lasting impression of Malta is of an island whose strength was its unity and singleness of purpose. This produced an invincible defence and a formidable offence.

In conclusion I would like to pay tribute to the original fighter pilots who did not survive the war. Peter Keeble, who was killed in one of the Gladiators. Timber Woods, who later was shot down in Greece. Jock Martin, who was missing during a Bomber Command attack on Germany shortly after his return from Malta. And to Alex, who was killed later during operations from Gibraltar. John Waters and Peter Hartley remain – they have left the Royal Air Force now and wherever they are I wish them well.

Finally, during my four and a half years in the island I met many of her people and I would like to take this opportunity of once again saying to them "saha".'

Let these words say all that we could have said in this book, had space permitted, of the unsurpassed bravery, skill and determination of all, Army, Navy and civilian, who were in the fight for Malta and the cause of freedom. If we have singled out here one single theme of heroism drawn from only one of the Services, let this be in no way a reflection upon the others. The telling of all the stories would take many books.

All the main figures in the Faith, Hope and Charity story mentioned in this book who survived the war rose to high rank. In fact, five of them are Wing Commanders, two of them having left the Service with that rank and the others at present holding it as serving officers.

Of the three surviving members of the original Station Fighter Flight, one is still with the Royal Air Force; Wing Commander George Burges is, at the time of writing, in command of a flying-boat unit in Singapore.

Wing Commander Collins, the man who more than any other helped to keep 'Faith', 'Hope' and 'Charity' flying, was eventually awarded the MBE for his services in the air defence of Malta, and retired from the Air Force after the war.

Wing Commander Dimmer is at the time of writing a Senior Technical Officer in the Middle East.

John Waters, now in business, left the Air Force as a Wing Commander after the war and would give anything, he says, to be able to fly a Gladiator once more.

Wing Commander Peter Hartley left the Air Force in 1947. He realised his ambition, and now has a farm in Cambridgeshire. Looking back on those epic days in Malta, he says, rather wistfully, 'It was a starry-eyed period. That's the word for it – starry-eyed.'

Warburton's War

Tony Spooner

Adrian Warburton was one of the most decorated pilots of
World War II. A below average misfit, Warburton was sent
to Malta to avoid trouble in the UK. Known at first as a
loner, when given his head, his spectacular results enabled
his unconventional behaviour to be overlooked.

Becoming CO of 69 Squadron, then 683 PR Squadron
'Warby' was fearless in the air, shooting down nine enemy
aircraft and winning fame in Malta for his invaluable photo-
reconnaissance work at Taranto. Based on interviews with
his colleagues, *Warburton's War*, paints a picture of a
fascinating man who with 350 operational missions from
Malta alone, became a living legend.

204 pages, 'B' format paperback

20pp b&w photograph sections

9 780907 579434 £7.99

Faith Hope and Malta GC

Ground and Air Heroes of the George Cross Island

Tony Spooner

Malta was a vital base from which Allied aircraft could inflict serious damage on the crucial Axis supply route to Rommel in North Africa. In order to secure that route the might of the Luftwaffe and Italian Air Forces were thrown together against the tiny island, affecting not just the defending servicemen and women but the entire population. Heavily bombed and running short of fuel and food, the island laboured to stand firm in the face of the enemy.

Faith, Hope and Malta GC vividly describes how the RAF and FAA fighter, bomber, torpedo and reconnaissance aircraft crews took the fight to the enemy and triumphantly succeeded with every odd stacked against them.

The exploits of, amongst others, 'Screwball' Buerling, Warburton, Broom and Gibbs are related together with extracts from diaries kept by some of the air and groundcrew involved.

Finally awarded the George Cross for its heroism and devotion to duty, the island fortress of Malta and its people played a key role in the Allied success of WWII and *Faith, Hope and Malta GC* provides a moving insight into those dark times using the words of those who were there.

208 pages 'B' format paperback

12 page b&w photograph section

9 780907 579588 £6.99

Pedestal

Peter C Smith

In the summer of 1942 one of the main issues in the balance was the fate of Malta. The island was still a bastion of the Royal Navy in the Mediterranean and a constant threat to the supply route for the enemy land forces in North Africa.

Malta bravely resisted every onslaught of the Axis powers, but food supplies and fuel oils were desperately short. In August of that year Operation Pedestal was launched – a last attempt to relieve Malta. Fourteen merchant ships were allocated to it and the Royal Navy provided the most powerful force ever to escort a convoy including four aircraft carriers.

Operating from Sardinia and Sicily, the Germans and Italians let fly with their shore-based aircraft on an unprecedented scale. The losses on the British side were appalling, but the objective was achieved and the blockade of Malta was finally lifted.

Told through the eyes of people who were there, Pedestal provides a gripping insight into the fight to keep Malta alive.

224 pages, 'B' format paperback
24 page b&w photograph section
9 780907 579199 £6.99

Eagles War

Peter C Smith

HMS Eagle was already old when war was declared in September 1939 and her Swordfish biplanes were soon flying escort to vital Australian troop convoys in the wastes of the Indian Ocean. When the war moved to the Mediterranean, Eagle's meagre air group bolstered by a few Sea Gladiator biplanes held the ring with Cunningham's superb fleet through the dark days of 1940 to 1941. Her aircraft took part in the naval victories of Calabria and Taranto; worked from desert air strips with great success and hounded the Italian Navy out of the Red Sea.

Following further ocean patrols in the South Atlantic, Eagle joined the famous Force 'H' at Gibraltar and did more than any other ship to sustain Malta during the islands' greatest ordeal, before being lost in action during the greatest of all convoy battles Operation Pedestal, in August 1942.

This almost day-by-day account of her battles and actions as seen through the eyes of its former crew members is a fitting tribute to all who served aboard her or flew from her decks.

192 pages, 'B' format paperback
b&w photograph section
9 780907 579533 £7.99

WWII paperback titles from Crécy Publishing

Enemy Coast Ahead

Guy Gibson VC, DSO and Bar, DFC and Bar

Wing Commander Guy Gibson gives one of the most brilliant descriptions of the Dambusters raid by the Lancasters of 617 Squadron which he himself led.

256 pages, paperback, photograph section

9 780907 579625 £6.99

Evader

Denys Teare

A story of escape and evasion behind enemy lines.

240 pages, paperback b&w photograph section

9 780907 579485 £6.99

Keeping Watch

Pip Beck

The story of an R/T operator in Bomber Command who talked down bomber crews returning from operations, met them off-duty and, all too often, mourned their loss.

192 pages, paperback, photograph section

9 780907 579380 £6.99

Lancaster Target

Jack Currie

The classic story of one crew's fight to survive a full tour of operations in the night skies of wartime Europe. Flying Lancaster bombers from RAF Wickenby, Jack Currie chronicles the life and death struggles against flak, night fighters and perilous weather.

192 pages, paperback, photograph section

9 780907 579281 £6.99

Mosquito Victory

Jack Currie

This sequel to Lancaster Target graphically and humorously describes all aspects of life as a WWII RAF bomber pilot on 'rest'. Mess life and antics intermingle with Jack's real task of instructing trainees on the four-engined Halifax bomber and his subsequent return to the élite Pathfinder force flying Mosquitoes of 1409 Weather Flight.

176 pages, paperback, photograph section

9 780907 579335 £6.99

Night Fighter

CF Rawnsley and Robert Wright

With John "Cat's-Eyes" Cunningham, "Jimmy" Rawnsley was half of one of the RAF's leading night fighter crews, destroying over twenty enemy aircraft.

256 pages, paperback, photograph section

9 780907 579670 £5.99

WWII paperback titles from Crécy Publishing

Night Flyer

Lewis Brandon DSO, DFC and Bar

The exciting story of one of the most successful RAF night fighting partnerships of the war, Night Flyer also charts the development of night fighting.

208 pages, paperback, photograph section

9 780907 579779 £5.99

Nine Lives

Al Deere

The renowned autobiography of New Zealand's most famous RAF pilot from the Munich crisis until the invasion of France in 1944. Al Deere experienced the drama of the early days of the Battle of Britain while operating with Spitfire squadrons based at Hornchurch and Manston, and his compelling story tells of the successes and frustrations during those critical weeks.

288 pages, paperback, photograph section

9 780907 579823 £7.99

No Moon Tonight

Don Charlwood

A Bomber Command classic, this is the breathtaking story of a wartime bomber crew facing the nightly bombing of the most strongly defended targets in Nazi Germany.

224 pages, paperback, photograph section

9 780907 579977 £6.99

Pathfinder

Air Vice-Marshal Don Bennett CB, CBE, DSO

The autobiography of the leader of the Pathfinders – the élite force designed to carry out pioneering target-marking and precision-bombing of Nazi-occupied Europe.

272 pages, paperback, photograph section

9 780907 579571 £5.99

Rear Gunner Pathfinders

Ron Smith DFM

The story of the air war over Germany as seen from the small perspex bubble of a 'Tail-End Charlie' rear gunner in a Lancaster.

200 pages, paperback, photograph section

9 780907 579274 £6.99

Uncommon Valour

AG Goulding DFM

A comprehensive account of Bomber Command's part in the Second World War, together with a personal view of the leadership of the force in those crucial years.

192 pages, paperback, photograph section

9 780859 790956 £4.99

WWII paperback titles from Crécy Publishing

Wing Leader

Air Vice-Marshal "Johnnie" Johnson CB, CBE, DSO and Two Bars, DFC and Bar

The thrilling story of the top-scoring Allied fighter pilot of World War Two 'Johnnie' Johnson.

320 pages, paperback, photograph section

9 780907 579878 £7.99

Wings Aflame

Doug Stokes

The acclaimed biography of Victor Beamish, the legendary Irish station commander who flew an incredible 126 fighter sorties in the Battle of Britain.

224 pages, paperback , photograph section

9 780907 579724 £5.99

Wings Over Georgia

Jack Currie

Forerunner to the best-selling Lancaster Target, the story of Jack Currie's early training in the UK, followed by a period with the US Army Air Corps and his return to England to join Bomber Command.

156 pages, paperback, photograph section

9 780907 579113 £3.99

Crecy Publishing Ltd,

1a Ringway Trading Estate, Shadowmoss Road, Manchester M22 5LH, UK

Tel: 0161 499 0024
Fax: 0161 499 0298

sales@crecy.co.uk

Order online at

www.crecy.co.uk